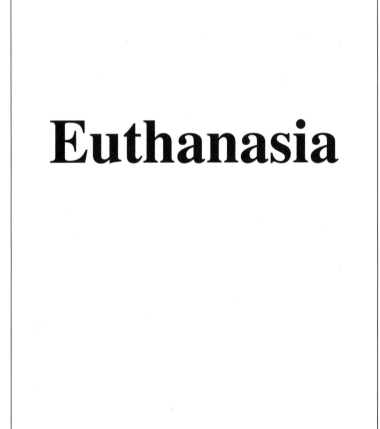

Euthanasia

Look for these and other books in the Lucent
Overview series:

Euthanasia

by Sunni Bloyd

LUCENT
B·O·O·K·S

LUCENT *Overview Series*

LUCENT Overview Series

Library of Congress Cataloging-in-Publication Data

Bloyd, Sunni.
    Euthanasia / by Sunni Bloyd.
        p.   cm. — (Lucent overview series)
    Includes bibliographical references and index.
    ISBN 1-56006-141-3 (alk. paper)
    1. Euthanasia—Juvenile literature.   [1. Euthanasia.]   I. Title.
II. Series.
R726.B57   1995
179'.7—dc20
                                      95-1332
                                          CIP
                                          AC

Copyright © 1995 by Lucent Books, Inc.
P.O. Box 289011, San Diego, CA 92198-9011
Printed in the U.S.A.

In memory of departed loved ones:
Marjorie, Alvin, Laura, Donald, Betty, and LeRoy

Acknowledgments

The author would like to express her appreciation to those who provided assistance and information during the preparation of this book:

Roger Purdy, California Medical Association; Arnie Collins, American Medical Association; Cynthia Smith; Victoria McKenna; John P. Eno; Claudia Stein; Linda Fuller; Janet McDonald; Marilynn Bates; Tom Willard; Paul di Tullio; Stephanie L. Posello, The Hastings Center; Judie Brown, American Life League, Inc.; Julia Curry and Mary L. Meyer, Choice in Dying; Reverend Paul Marks, O.S.B., Human Life International; John A. Pridonoff, Diana Smith, and Kris Larson, Hemlock Society; the ARC: Association for Retarded Citizens of the United States; Robert L. Risley, Americans Against Human Suffering; Minnesota Citizens Concerned for Life; Jack Nicholl, Californians Against Human Suffering; American Life Lobby; TASH: The Association for Persons with Severe Handicaps; the staff of Orange Public Library; John and Jeremy Bloyd; and especially my editor, Lori Shein.

Contents

Introduction

EVERY YEAR IN THE United States two million people die. Most people have known someone who has died—a neighbor, a friend, a family member. Death, like birth, is an experience no human being can avoid. Yet in the past century in technologically advanced countries there have been dramatic changes in how and where people die.

Changes in how and where people die

Until about 1900, decisions about what medical treatment an ill patient received were seldom difficult or ambiguous. Doctors had few choices. For most patients, a serious illness meant swift, certain death.

Scientific research since the turn of the century has yielded new, exciting options for doctors and other caregivers. Since the advent of vaccines and antibiotics, contagious diseases like influenza and pneumonia, the leading causes of death in 1900, are no longer major killers. Today long-term, degenerative diseases like cancer and heart disease are among the most common causes of death in the United States. But even these diseases can often be controlled. Recent medical advances allow people with chronic or terminal illnesses to live much longer.

Just as the past century has produced changes in how people die, the places people die have also

(Opposite page) The death of a loved one is a sad event, and coping with the loss can be extremely difficult. As euthanasia involves the decision to end a life, it is a subject that naturally provokes debate.

changed. For most of history, people usually died at home. In the United States today 80 percent of deaths take place in hospitals or nursing homes. Although patients often benefit from the care and services provided by hospitals, this distancing of the dying from the home has affected the way Americans think and feel about death.

Changing attitudes towards death

Social scientist Lewis Thomas studied changes in attitudes towards death over the last two centuries. He writes, "[Before this century] everyone knew about death at first hand. There was nothing unfamiliar or even queer about the phenomenon. People seem to have known a lot more about the process itself than is the case today. The 'deathbed' was a real place, and the dying person usually knew where he was and when it was time to assemble the family and call for the priest."

Americans are no longer familiar with death firsthand. They have seen thousands of fictional and real deaths on television and movie screens, but few have ever been present at another person's death. Some experts suggest Americans fear death because they do not recognize it as a normal part of life.

Moreover, because modern medicine routinely produces results and recoveries that may seem miraculous, Americans generally expect every health crisis to have a happy ending. Even doctors sometimes regard death as a medical failure instead of a natural event. Lewis Thomas describes how doctors today often react to death. "Patients known to be dying are segregated as much as possible from all the others, and doctors spend as little time in attendance as they can manage. Although they are familiar with the business, seeing more of it at first hand than anyone else in our kind of society, they never become

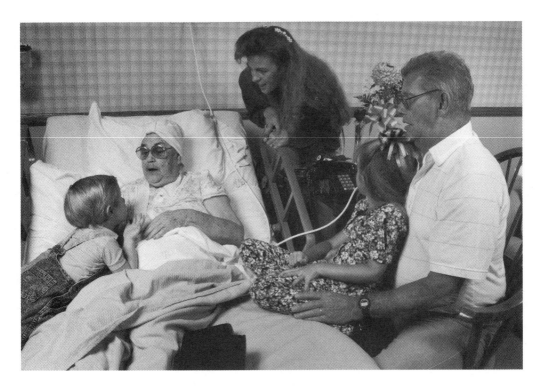

used to it. Death is shocking, dismaying, even terrifying. A dying patient is a kind of freak. It is the most unacceptable of all abnormalities, an offense against nature itself."

The role of technology

In their efforts to stave off death, doctors rely more and more on the technological wonders of the twentieth century. Hospitals now have the means to take over the functioning of nearly every vital organ in the human body. Machines called life support systems can regulate breathing, maintain a heartbeat, deliver nourishment, and filter wastes from a patient's kidneys. Other machines can restart stopped hearts.

These marvels of modern technology can play a vital role in recovery following surgery or serious illness. And medical technology can sometimes extend life even when it cannot cure fatal

A dying cancer patient spends precious time with family members. As the majority of deaths now occur outside the home, away from family, Americans are becoming increasingly unfamiliar and uncomfortable with death.

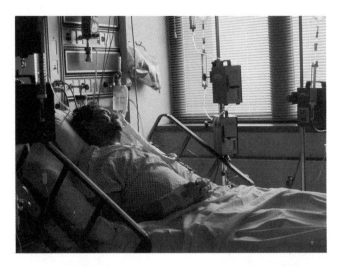

A patient in an intensive care unit is kept alive with the aid of a respirator.

diseases like AIDS or some forms of cancer. But in the final stages of diseases such as these medical technology can also be viewed as merely prolonging the dying process.

Thomas Murray of Case Western Reserve University specializes in ethics—standards of behavior and moral judgment. He explains that many people have come to fear a long and painful dying more than they fear death itself. "Americans today have a horror of prolonged dying," he says. "They are repelled by the thought of dying completely out of control, tethered to machines, perhaps in a lot of pain, perhaps in a kind of dazed twilight. They want to avoid that at all costs."

Divided feelings

The different and sometimes opposing ways members of a society view death—and life—drive the euthanasia debate. For, at its simplest, euthanasia involves the decision to end life. Even in the most terrible of circumstances, when death is seen as providing desperately needed relief, the act of ending a life causes grave concern.

Society's divided feelings about euthanasia are reflected in the words of a sixteenth-century surgeon. Ambroise Paré was traveling with the French army in 1537 when he encountered this scene, recorded in his diary:

> After the battle, we thronged into the city and passed over the dead bodies and some that were not dead yet, hearing them cry under the feet of our horses, which made a great pity in my heart, and truly I repented that I had gone forth from Paris to see so pitiful a spectacle. Being in the city, I entered a stable, thinking to lodge my horse. . . . [There] I found four dead soldiers and three [dying soldiers] who were propped against the wall, their faces wholly disfigured, and they neither saw, nor heard, nor spoke, and their clothes were still flaming from the gun powder, which had burned them.

> Beholding them with pity there came an old soldier who asked me if there was any means of curing them. I told him no. At once he approached them and cut their throats gently and without anger. Seeing this great cruelty I said to him that he was an evil man. He answered me that he prayed God that when he should be in such a case, he might find someone that would do the same for him, so that he might not languish miserably.

The debate over euthanasia is, understandably, clouded by emotion and many different points of view. Obviously no single solution applies to all situations. So exploring the full range of possibilities is essential for readers to understand the issue and reach informed opinions of their own. For while euthanasia will continue to be the subject of political and public debate for a long time, it may someday be of profound personal relevance to each individual as well.

1

What Is Euthanasia and Why Is It So Troubling?

EUTHANASIA, WHAT SOME people call mercy killing, is one of the most controversial and emotional issues of our time. The subject of euthanasia provokes strong emotions because it involves ending a human life, a taboo in our culture under most circumstances.

Is it right to end life prematurely?

The word *euthanasia* comes from ancient Greece. It is a combination of words meaning good or happy (*eu*) and death (*thanatos*). Euthanasia is the act of killing someone or permitting or helping someone to die for reasons of mercy. Usually it involves a person who is gravely ill or injured, and dying or near death. The purpose of euthanasia is to prevent or end suffering resulting from an illness or injury. But this purpose is itself part of the controversy surrounding euthanasia. For it leads directly to the question: Is it ever right to cut life short? On one hand, traditional morality and medical teaching say it is never right to kill an innocent person. On the other, advocates of euthanasia say that there

(Opposite page) Euthanasia is controversial even when it involves putting an end to the suffering of a dying person. Some people believe that it is never acceptable to cut short a human life.

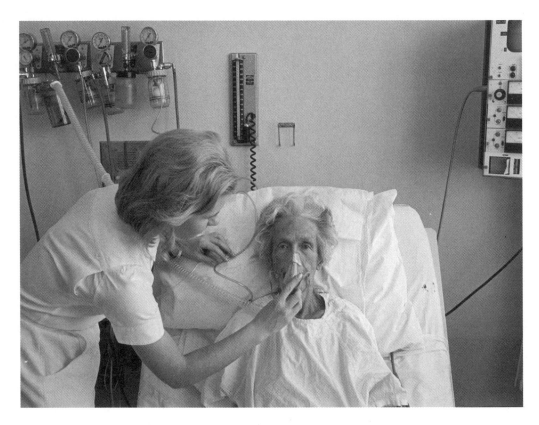

Many people fear being forced to endure a prolonged, painful death, tethered to machines.

are times when bringing about another person's death is a compassionate act.

Psychiatrist Walter Reich expresses the feelings of many people who oppose euthanasia. "Mercy killing is still killing," he says, "and it corrupts the value of life. . . . A patient, no matter how ill or despondent, is still human and still alive, and killing that patient, no matter what the law says or what the circumstances are, is still killing."

Reich feels that legalizing euthanasia would change society for the worse. "People kill without benefit of the law every day," he says. "Soldiers kill other soldiers legally. But societies can experience such killings and remain essentially decent. It's when they legalize the killings of their own innocent members that they remove an obstacle that blocks the all-too-easy slide of civilization into moral chaos."

Supporters of euthanasia say that there is a difference between killing someone and helping a person die. They argue that it is all right to help someone end his or her life, as long as that person has a good reason for it.

David Lewis, an AIDS counselor in Vancouver, British Columbia, has assisted in the deaths of eight AIDS-afflicted friends. He says, "People at that terminal phase in their lives should be able to say, 'It is enough. I don't want to suffer anymore. I want to die.' To refuse to help them would be criminal."

Passive euthanasia

Most cases of euthanasia happen without controversy. Patients who are very ill tell their doctors that they do not want to be kept on life support or revived if their heart stops. They may sign legal documents that authorize doctors or family members to see that their wishes are carried out. Then, when death approaches, doctors "allow" their patients to die. This is known as passive euthanasia, because it does not involve taking any actions that directly cause death.

Sometimes, when patients are incapable of speaking for themselves, family members must decide whether to disconnect life support. This, too, is a type of passive euthanasia. Doctors and family discuss what treatment is possible and what the long-term chances for survival are, and then a decision is reached based on what the patient would have decided.

Passive euthanasia takes place every day in thousands of hospitals across the United States. It is not illegal. Authoritative medical bodies like the American Medical Association (AMA) approve of it, as do most religious authorities.

"Passive . . . euthanasia is not euthanasia (mercy killing) at all, but merely the avoidance or discontinuation of *extraordinary* means of preserving life," explains one expert on ethics, the study of moral behavior. "Passive euthanasia, so called, is moral, legal and ethical. It is, in fact, a necessary part of every good doctor's concern for his patient's welfare and is standard procedure in every good hospital."

When nothing else can be done

The story of Jill Weatherford is typical of many cases of passive euthanasia. Jill was baby-sitting her infant granddaughter in June 1993 when she collapsed with a massive stroke. Her husband, Larry, found her unconscious when he came home from work that evening. He immediately called for emergency medical assistance, but Jill had already suffered extensive brain damage.

At the hospital, doctors put the comatose Jill on life support. A respirator helped her breathe. She received antibiotics and fluids intravenously (directly into the bloodstream via a needle inserted into a vein) and nutrients through a tube inserted into her nose. Thus she remained, her condition unchanged, for two months.

In August Jill's doctors told Larry that they had done all they could. They were convinced Jill would never emerge from her coma. They wanted to take her off the respirator and discontinue the antibiotics. "Jill will probably die of pneumonia," one doctor told Larry. "That often happens when life support is removed."

Larry discussed the doctors' prognoses with his family. Everyone agreed that Jill would not have wanted to live indefinitely on a respirator. A few days later the respirator was shut off and antibiotics were discontinued. Jill died of pneumonia in her sleep four months later. Larry does not regret shutting off the respirator. "Jill was already gone," he told friends shortly after her death.

A merciful death

Far more controversial is the procedure known as active euthanasia. In active euthanasia, death is the direct result of steps taken by a doctor, family member, or friend. The most common type of active euthanasia occurs when a person with a painful, incurable disease asks a doctor for help in dying. The doctor gives the patient a prescription for a drug that will cause death and instructs the patient on its use. The patient can then take the drug in private when he or she chooses. This type of euthanasia is known as assisted suicide.

Because it is illegal, most cases of assisted suicide are kept secret. However, many experts in medical ethics consider it a moral act when the doctor has known the patient for a long time and the patient faces a prolonged, painful death. In 1991 Dr. Timothy Quill risked prosecution for murder by publicizing his role in one patient's suicide.

Quill wrote in the *New England Journal of Medicine* about a patient he called "Diane." He had treated Diane, a forty-five-year-old leukemia patient, for eight years. By the spring of 1990 there was little more he could do for her. The only remaining treatment was extremely painful and offered only a 25 percent chance of success. Diane decided that she did not want the treatment. Instead she asked Quill to help her die. Quill gave her a strong sedative and told her how to use it. Within a few days, Diane ended her life.

When the article was published, few people criticized Quill. Specialists in medical ethics praised his compassion. "Dr. Quill and Diane had a long-standing relationship characterized by mutual admiration and trust," one professor of

Dr. Timothy Quill published an article about his experience assisting in the suicide of a leukemia patient. Most people praised Quill's actions as compassionate.

religious studies wrote. "He could be merciful to Diane because he knew her and related to her as a friend." Given physicians' tendency toward conservative care, it is likely that most assisted suicides practiced in the United States follow this pattern.

"It's over, Debbie"

A few cases each year involve ending a life by direct action. A doctor, family member, or friend will administer a lethal dose of drugs, or use other means to kill someone who is suffering. Usually this occurs when the sick person is incapable of taking these measures by himself or herself.

The Journal of the American Medical Association printed one doctor's anonymous account of one such killing performed in 1988. The doctor said he had been called to the hospital bed of a young woman named Debbie while he was still in medical school. Debbie was dying of cancer. After many months of sickness she weighed only eighty pounds. She struggled to breathe and was obviously in terrible pain. The young doctor could see from her chart that she was not responding to treatment.

Debbie whispered something, so he bent down to hear her. Even up close he could hardly make out her words. "Let's get this over with," she said faintly. Without a word the doctor filled a syringe with a powerful painkiller and injected it into Debbie. Four minutes later she was dead. "It's over, Debbie," the young doctor said softly to the dead woman.

In this case, the doctor's story aroused a storm of controversy. Some readers praised the journal for publishing the article, saying the issue it raised, whether doctors should perform active euthanasia, ought to be discussed. Other readers

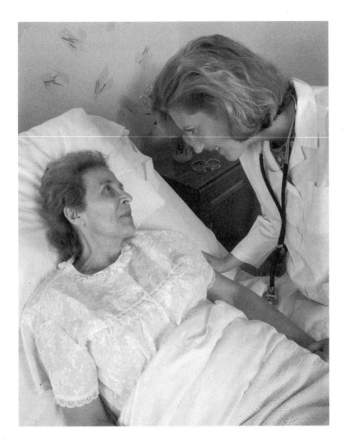

Some doctors believe that the special bond of trust that they share with their patients would be broken if they performed active euthanasia.

condemned mercy killing or objected to the impersonal nature of the death. Even supporters of euthanasia criticized the young doctor for being so quick to kill someone he did not know well.

Objections to active euthanasia

Many physicians object to the idea of killing their patients. They say that the special bond of trust between patients and their physicians would be destroyed if doctors performed active euthanasia.

"I believe it would be harmful to the medical profession," says Dr. Douglas Kinsella, a professor of medical ethics at the University of Calgary in Canada. "It transgresses one of our basic moral principles: Don't kill."

Samuel F. Hunter, a student at the University of Texas Medical School at Galveston, wrote an essay on the subject that appeared in the *Journal of the American Medical Association*. In it he argues that society would lose faith in doctors if they performed active euthanasia, and urges his fellow physicians to improve traditional medical skills instead of killing their patients:

> Instead of promoting active euthanasia, we can best serve our patients by accurate [diagnosis of their condition] and skillful management of complications and pain. Along with social workers and the clergy, we can bolster emotional strength. When we no longer heal, we [ease pain] and comfort. This has been the time-honored tradition of medicine. Adding death-on-demand to our armamentarium would subvert society's faith in us.

The thinning line between passive and active euthanasia

Part of the euthanasia controversy arises over drawing the line between passive and active euthanasia. It is not always easy to tell the difference between the two.

For example, it is difficult to tell the difference between passive and active euthanasia when the subject is in a state of permanent unconsciousness. In cases where a patient's brain has lost all ability to function, removal of life support is quickly followed by death. But in some patients, like Jill Weatherford, only the parts of the brain responsible for thinking and independent action die. The brain stem remains alive, but the patient will never regain consciousness.

Like Jill Weatherford, many of these severely impaired patients are able to breathe for themselves if life support is removed. They are awake, but unaware. It is estimated that there are ten thousand permanently unconscious patients in nursing homes across America. Properly cared for and given nutrition and water through feeding tubes, they can survive as long as thirty years. Withdraw feeding tubes, and most of these patients would die from lack of food and water within ten days.

Since 1986 the AMA has classified withdrawal of tube feeding as an acceptable form of passive euthanasia, along with actions such as disconnecting a respirator or not trying to revive a patient whose heart has failed. Doctors may ethically withdraw tube nourishment and liquids from patients according to AMA guidelines, once it has been established that the patient is in an irreversible state of unconsciousness.

Many doctors support the AMA position on tube feeding. In situations where the patient is unconscious and doctors predict no chance of

recovery, feeding tubes serve the same general purpose as other forms of life support technology. Says Dr. Nancy W. Dickey, head of the AMA's Ethics Council: "The person is being kept alive artificially by technology. All we're talking about is withdrawing the technology."

This view is not shared by all doctors. Withdrawal of feeding tubes leads to death by starvation and dehydration, not by disease or injury. This difference troubles those who oppose feeding tube removal. They believe it is wrong to cause the death of someone who maintains a heartbeat and breathes without assistance.

"Food and [fluids] represent the basic care all patients should have, regardless of the underlying illness," says Basile J. Uddo, a lawyer specializing in medical issues. "In some situations, nutrition and water may not have a curative effect. However, the absence or presence of a curative effect is not relevant because the purpose is to comfort and care for the patient. A person's need for care and comfort does not diminish with age. Nor does it diminish if a person is dying. On the contrary, it is the dying patient who most requires our care during the last days."

Members of the medical profession, trained to preserve life, must make perhaps the most troubling decisions. Medical tradition and training stress doctors' responsibility to act in their patients' best interests. But what should be done for a patient whose only release from suffering is death?

The oath of Hippocrates

As they begin their medical career, many young doctors take an oath first written by Hippocrates, a Greek physician of the fifth century B.C. With the oath they promise to do nothing that will harm their patient, and never to administer lethal drugs.

New doctors swear, "I will follow that method of treatment which, according to my ability and judgment, I consider for the benefit of my patient, and abstain from whatever is [harmful] and wrong. I will give no deadly medicine to anyone, even if asked, nor suggest any such counsel."

The oath of Hippocrates established a standard of behavior for the medical profession. But it was written in a time when most patients either died or got better. Modern doctors have an undreamed-of array of life-prolonging drugs and technologies to call on, but they must bear the awesome responsibility of making life-or-death decisions in cases in which the patient is not going to get better but might be kept alive for a long time.

Many thoughtful doctors have pointed out that, while the oath does include a ban on killing patients, it also calls for doctors to do only that which will benefit those in their care. They argue that keeping patients alive when their quality of life is poor does not benefit the patient.

"A misguided medical profession"

Dr. Jack Kevorkian, a Michigan physician, has openly helped more than twenty people take their own lives since 1990. He considers a doctor's responsibility to his or her patients more important than any rules set down by the oath of Hippocrates. He says:

> A misguided medical profession has for centuries been responsible for much unnecessary suffering and personal degradation by refusing to hasten a merciful death for pleading patients. To me it is incredible that a doctor could abide the agony of a doomed human simply because of a personal commitment to an invented abstraction [like the oath of Hippocrates].

The debate over these conflicting responsibilities is not likely to be resolved soon. Meanwhile, doctors will continue to be troubled by the difficult decisions they must make.

Worry and confusion over the death of a loved one

Family and friends of dying people find the idea of euthanasia no less troubling than do physicians. It is hard to determine the right thing to do, especially since their decision could mean the death of someone they love. Sometimes what the dying person would have wanted done is uncertain. Even when the dying person is able to make the decision unassisted, someone in the family often disagrees. All of these conflicts are heightened by the grief that accompanies the loss of someone dear.

Dr. Jack Kevorkian has publicly aided in the deaths of more than twenty people. He poses here with two women who later took their lives with his assistance.

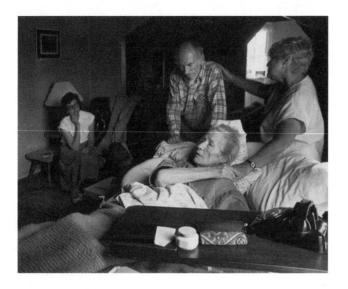

A woman who is dying of cancer and her husband find comfort from a social worker's home visit. This kind of support can lessen the desire for a quick ending.

Arjen Eric, the brother of a Dutch man who chose euthanasia, describes his feelings during the last days of his brother's life. "When you are not with him, it is much more difficult," he says. "All kinds of thoughts continuously come to mind. This is the last evening together, this is the last time I will walk through this corridor with him still being there. . . .

"People have to know that [euthanasia] does not just affect the dying person. They have to know how difficult it is for all of us. It was a tremendous strain."

Euthanasia is a tremendous strain, even for those who do not have to make the difficult decision. Euthanasia elicits strong responses because it involves life and death, and brings into question values placed on life and death.

As medical technology finds new ways of extending life, new controversies over their use will arise. With medical tradition and training on one side, rebels like Jack Kevorkian on the other, and the terminally ill in the middle, the growing debate over euthanasia clearly will continue to be painful and emotionally charged.

JACK
the
DEATH WITH DIGNITY, the ULTIMATE CIVIL RIGHT!
JACK
the

2

The Right to Die

NOWHERE IN THE Constitution's list of basic human rights is it written that an individual has a right to die. However, the right to choose one's own time of death—whether by suicide, by refusing medical treatment, or by discontinuing treatment—is central to the euthanasia debate. This choice is commonly referred to as the right to die.

Life cannot and should not be maintained indefinitely

Although some religious faiths expressly prohibit suicide, most recognize that life cannot and should not be maintained indefinitely. Pope Pius XII set forth this view of passive euthanasia in 1957, in a paper titled "The Prolongation of Life." The pope explained that every family ought to use "ordinary means of care"—care that gives comfort and encourages recovery. But extraordinary means of care, such as a respirator, may be discontinued after it becomes obvious that the patient is not benefiting from them.

In 1980 Pope John Paul II commented, "When inevitable death is imminent in spite of the means used, it is permitted to . . . refuse forms of treatment that would only secure a precarious and

(Opposite page) Supporters of Dr. Kevorkian rally for the legalization of assisted suicide. Although the right to die with dignity is not expressly written in the Constitution, many people feel that it is a basic human right.

Pope Pius XII expressed support of passive euthanasia in a 1957 paper titled "The Prolongation of Life."

burdensome prolongation of life, so long as the normal care due to a sick person in similar cases is not interrupted."

Jewish belief, too, requires continuing care for the sick but does not require the dying process to be prolonged. The Talmud, the book of Jewish law and tradition, specifically states that artificial means of postponing the death process may be removed. "By allowing death to come when it is imminent, a person is hardly denying [divine will]," writes Jewish religious author Seymour Siegel in the journal *Sh'ma*. "He is permitting God's judgment to take its effect, without the intervention of useless, artificial means. . . . The mere functioning of physical systems is not the ultimate good."

In the patient's best interest

The difficulty arises in determining when that period of "burdensome prolongation of life" has arrived. Most doctors are guided by the best interest principle. This principle originates in the portion of the oath of Hippocrates that states, "I will follow that method of treatment which, according to my ability and judgment, I consider for the benefit of my patient." Doctors are required to do what is best for each patient.

This requirement is backed up by serious penalties for those who ignore it. Physicians who fail to provide adequate care face criminal prosecution for negligence or even murder. They can lose their license to practice medicine, or be sued for malpractice. Thus, doctors have both pragmatic and philosophical reasons to take a patient's best interest seriously.

And many do. But this does not necessarily lead to agreement about what actions serve the patient's best interest. Nor is there agreement on when—or if—a patient has a right to die.

It WOULD Be CRUEL to PROLONG the iNeVitaBLe.

It'S iNeVitaBLe to PROLONG the CRueLtY.

Today many doctors believe it is more ethical to permit the death of hopelessly ill patients than to prolong life by using all the technological tools at their disposal. "There is a time and place where prolonging human suffering is not doing my job as a physician," says George A. Perera, former dean of the Columbia Medical School.

But other doctors believe they should continue to fight for a patient until the very end. Says Dr. Marshall Brumer of Ft. Lauderdale, Florida: "The doctor's responsibility is to do everything he can to sustain lives. . . . To stand idly by and watch a person die is intolerable."

Legal issues involving the right to die

Before the courts gave guidance on right-to-die issues, doctors mostly relied on the idea of a patient's best interest to make decisions about withdrawing or withholding treatment. Most doctors assumed that it was always in a patient's best interest to choose life over death. Patients could do little to oppose a doctor who forced unwanted medical procedures on them. Then a series of court cases established an individual's right to refuse medical treatment.

The first cases, argued in the 1970s, involved blood transfusions. Some religions forbid transfusions even when death is inevitable without them. But when hospitalized followers refused transfusions, doctors often performed the procedure anyway, convinced that their obligation to save lives took priority over the patients' beliefs. A number of these patients sued. They argued that a competent person has the right to refuse medical treatment even though death may result. The issue became known then as the right to die.

No clear precedent emerged in these early cases. Some courts declared that the right to refuse treatment was justified as an aspect of religious freedom. Others concluded that the state's interest in preserving life took higher priority. The controversy continued until 1976, when the courts reached a final decision in the case of Karen Ann Quinlan.

Karen Ann Quinlan

In 1975 twenty-one-year-old Karen Ann Quinlan was discovered in a coma after an overdose of drugs and alcohol. Doctors placed Karen on a respirator. She did not regain consciousness; although her body responded to sound, light, and smell, the special set of characteristics that made up Karen Ann Quinlan was gone. She had suffered irreversible brain damage.

After three months, Karen's family accepted the fact that she would never recover. Her mother told those who inquired about Karen's condition,

In 1975 Karen Ann Quinlan entered a coma following an overdose of drugs and alcohol. When it became apparent that she would never recover, Quinlan's parents asked the hospital to take their daughter off the respirator.

"Our daughter is just a vegetable. She is not alive." Karen's parents asked doctors to remove her from the respirator.

Everyone thought Karen would die without the respirator to help her breathe. The doctors and hospital administrators, reasoning that removing the machine would be the same as killing her, refused to do it.

A right to die in peace

The Quinlans sued to force the hospital to honor their request. Their lawyers presented evidence that Karen's condition was hopeless. They argued that continued medical intervention in Karen's case was a violation of her privacy. The young woman had a right to die in peace, they

The Quinlans sued when the hospital refused to honor their request. The court decided in their favor, establishing several important legal precedents for other, similar cases.

said. Friends testified that before she fell into the coma Karen had said she would not want her life artificially sustained if she were terminally ill. Ultimately the New Jersey Supreme Court agreed with the Quinlans.

When doctors finally did remove Karen's respirator, she did not die as everyone had expected. Instead she lived for nine more years, given basic medical and nursing care and nourishment through a feeding tube. Finally, in June 1985 Karen Ann Quinlan died without ever regaining consciousness.

The Quinlan case became a legal landmark, consulted by nearly every court dealing with right-to-die issues. It set several important precedents. First, the case established the principle of informed consent, based on the idea that every adult has the right to decide what shall be done with his or her body. From this time on, doctors and hospitals could not perform medical procedures without explaining them and obtaining patients' consent. Furthermore, the decision recognized that a patient's best interest might not necessarily be continued life. The court accepted quality of life as an important consideration in determining when life support systems should be removed. Finally, the court gave families and doctors the right to make decisions about medical treatment when patients are legally incompetent, or unable to make decisions on their own behalf.

Seeking legal permission to die

Court cases had thus far established that a patient could refuse medical treatment, but many questions remained unaddressed. No one could say just how far the right to die extended. Must a doctor always honor a patient's wishes, or are there times when the doctor's judgment ought to prevail? What protection would medical workers have from charges of negligence or assisting suicide if they allowed a patient to die? These questions received national attention when a seventy-three-year-old man named Abe Perlmutter decided that he wanted to die.

In the spring of 1981 Abe Perlmutter was hospitalized with ALS, known as Lou Gehrig's disease, a condition that causes progressive wasting and paralysis of the muscles. He required a respirator to breathe. Shortly after Mr. Perlmutter went into the hospital, his wife died. Depressed by the loss, he tried to kill himself. Three times he attempted to take off his respirator. Three times doctors and nurses restrained him.

To make sure that no one in his family or on the hospital staff could be charged with wrongdoing in his death, Mr. Perlmutter sought a court order to turn off the respirator. His physician, Dr. Marshall Brumer, and the hospital opposed the

The children of Abe Perlmutter discuss their decision to support their father in his court battle for the right to die. Perlmutter sought a court order after several attempts to remove his own respirator were halted by hospital staff.

request. They contended that Mr. Perlmutter's suicidal thinking stemmed from depression over his wife's death and that he could live another two years with little pain from his illness.

In court Brumer argued that Abe Perlmutter was too depressed by his wife's death to really know what he wanted for himself. "Every hospital is filled with sick and depressed patients," he said. "Patients with these characteristics are easily susceptible to undue influence, harassment and brain washing. The premature death of patients should not be sanctioned by the court because of motivations ranging from . . . emotions to financial considerations."

There were numerous court hearings and appeals. Finally, in September 1981 the Florida Fourth District Court of Appeals ruled in favor of Mr. Perlmutter. He removed the respirator tube from his throat and died less than two days later.

Many physicians share Brumer's concerns. Dr. Marca L. Sipski, director of spinal cord injury services at the Kessler Institute for Rehabilitation in West Orange, New Jersey, treats people who are paralyzed as a result of accidents. Most of her patients are depressed and say they want to die—at first.

"In the first hours, days, and weeks they all want to die," she says. "When they're first admitted to the hospital they will tell us not to resuscitate them. . . . Yet we know that in a few months, when they see that life is not only possible but often good, they change their minds."

Solutions to the problem

The medical community has tried to find satisfactory ways of dealing with requests from patients who wish to die. One solution to this problem is to wait until the patient obtains a court order requiring the withdrawal of support systems,

People who are suddenly paralyzed as the result of accidents often become severely depressed and some express a desire to end their lives.

but this solution costs patients and their families considerable grief and expense. Another solution is to make a bargain with the patient. Dr. Andre Hellegers, director of the Kennedy Institute for the Study of Human Reproduction and Bioethics, remembers a woman who came to his hospital weekly to use the kidney machine. One day the seventy-year-old woman said she did not want to be hooked up to the machine. She said she wanted to die.

Hellegers says the request was especially troubling because kidney failure causes a kind of blood poisoning that clouds the mind. "We didn't know if she was telling us not to turn [the kidney machine] on, or if it was the disease talking," he explains. "So we said, 'We'll clean your blood once more. Then we'll say, "Was that your disease speaking or was that you?"'

"In some cases, the person says, 'No, it was my disease. Now I feel fine,'" Hellegers continues. But in this case, the woman's decision remained the same. Hellegers arranged for the patient to speak to several doctors, including psychologists. Then, when he was sure she remained committed to her decision, her wish was honored.

Advance directives

Although informal agreements like the one Hellegers made with his patient were sufficient in some cases, it became obvious that people needed a legally enforceable way to direct doctors to withdraw or withhold life-sustaining treatment in the event of terminal illness. A special kind of document was necessary because most legal directives expire when the person who authorized them becomes incompetent. This type of document is called an advance directive.

The first advance directive to deal with euthanasia was the living will, developed by Luis

Attorney Luis Kutner developed the living will, a document that states the signer's wish to be allowed to die rather than be kept alive by artificial means if there is little possibility of recovery.

Kutner of the Euthanasia Education Council in 1969. The living will is a document in which the signer requests to be allowed to die rather than be kept alive by artificial means if recovery is unlikely. It differs from a traditional will, which is a legal declaration of a person's wishes regarding disposal of property and belongings after death. Relatively few people showed interest in living wills until the Quinlan case captured national attention; the council distributed only 750,000 copies of the will between 1969 and 1975. In the year and a half after Karen Ann Quinlan became a famous name, however, the council received 1.25 million requests for copies of the will. Newspaper advice columnists Abigail Van Buren and Ann Landers distributed additional thousands.

According to Donald McKinney, president of the Euthanasia Education Council, the living will relieves family members and doctors of the responsibility for making extremely difficult decisions. "Its great value is that a tremendous burden of guilt is lifted from the family and children when a person signs the will. And it is also a great deal of help to doctors," he explains.

But while many authorities praise the living will, Joseph P. Meissner, president of the Cleveland Right to Life Society, calls it a "death warrant." The living will, he says, is a blank check that authorizes the ending of the signer's life with less protection for the signer than an ordinary sales contract.

"Laws now protect consumers from entering hasty or uninformed transactions," he argues. "Those charged with serious crimes must be read their rights before they can confess. How ironic it would be if the signer of a living will had less legal protection than the purchaser of a used car."

Even those who oppose living wills, however, agree that they stimulate communication among patients, their families, and their doctors. Dying patients report that the wills provide a sense of security and the feeling that they have regained control over their lives.

Natural death legislation

When they were first introduced, living wills did have several drawbacks. They were not recognized by any state as legal documents. Doctors could not be forced to follow them. Medical care providers were not protected from prosecution if they disconnected life support systems. Also, life insurance companies could claim that policyholders who died as a result of having their life support disconnected had committed suicide, and refuse to pay insurance benefits.

Laws were needed to establish a patient's right to die. In 1978 California became the first state to pass so-called natural death legislation. The

Last rights

California Natural Death Act provides legal backing to living wills. The act establishes that withdrawing or removing life-sustaining medical treatment is not suicide, and that doing so does not invalidate life insurance policies. It allows people over the age of eighteen to sign a declaration authorizing their doctor to withhold or withdraw treatment that "only prolongs the process of dying and is not necessary for comfort or to [ease] pain." Two witnesses who would not benefit from the death of the applicant must sign the declaration.

The California law served as a model for laws around the country. In 1991 Congress passed the U.S. Patient Self-Determination Act, requiring all hospitals, nursing homes, hospices, and home care programs receiving federal funds to brief patients on their rights and the way to terminate medical care. Today all fifty states recognize living wills or other forms of advance directives through laws like the California Natural Death Act.

Few living wills are in force

In spite of increased interest in living wills, the public proved slow to put them into effect. By 1987 only 9 percent of Americans had made a living will. In a 1987 study of California doctors working with terminally ill patients, more than a third reported they had no patients with a living will, and more than 70 percent said they had had fewer than five patients with a living will. In 1988 a ten-year review of the medical records of 186 patients likely to have a living will in Massachusetts General Hospital did not find a single mention of any kind of advance directive.

Despite their intended purpose, living wills do not guarantee that a patient's wishes will be fulfilled. Vague wording or lack of a proper signature may void the instructions in the will. Perhaps most importantly, the living will leaves the final

decision to the doctor. Family members cannot intervene if the doctor or other hospital staff choose a course that conflicts with the living will. These drawbacks may have contributed to the unpopularity of living wills.

Durable power of attorney

In 1983 a presidential commission looking into these problems recommended the creation of a special durable power of attorney for health care. A power of attorney is a document in which one person grants another person the power to perform certain acts on his or her behalf. For example, parents who leave their children at a child care center often fill out a power of attorney authorizing medical care for them in an emergency.

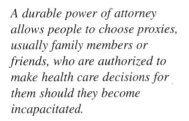

A durable power of attorney allows people to choose proxies, usually family members or friends, who are authorized to make health care decisions for them should they become incapacitated.

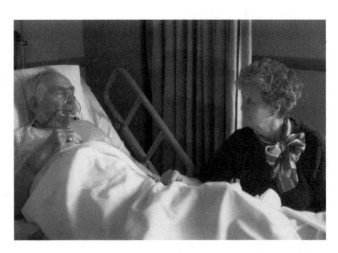

While the usual power of attorney expires if the person signing it becomes incapacitated, a durable power of attorney remains active. As a result, it provides a simple, flexible way of assuring health care decisions are made as incompetent patients would wish.

The durable power of attorney differs from the living will in three ways. First, it appoints a proxy, or agent, to make a person's health care decisions if he or she is incapacitated. Most likely the agent will be a family member or friend, someone who respects and understands the sick person's values and beliefs, rather than the attending physician, who may be a stranger. Second, the durable power of attorney is more than a rejection of treatment. It allows the agent to make all the sick person's health care decisions, considering a wide range of choices and selecting what is deemed best. Third, it allows the person signing it to be specific about what he or she wants. With a durable power of attorney, for example, it is possible to refuse use of a respirator but request continued administration of fluids or antibiotics.

Laws recognizing general durable powers of attorney exist in all fifty states. In 1986 the AMA created a model durable power of attorney for health care and urged its adoption in every state. Today thirteen states specifically authorize the use of durable powers of attorney for ending life-sustaining treatment. The Patient Self-Determination Act requires hospitals to tell people about their right to control their treatment through living wills and powers of attorney.

Drawbacks to delegated decision making

However, even durable powers of attorney have drawbacks. Delegated decision making may not anticipate the patient's wishes in all situations. While the agent may be a close friend of the sick person, perhaps there is no time to discuss the patient's preferences. Even when such a discussion takes place, it may be in such vague terms that the agent is not left adequately informed.

And obviously, the choice to actually end a life is more difficult to make than is an abstract agreement. A 1977 study found that willingness to withdraw life support decreases from 70 percent to 46 percent when a person must make the decision not for oneself, but for a loved one.

Controversy and good intentions

These unresolved issues ensure that controversy will continue over the right to die, even though some aspects, such as a patient's right to refuse treatment, are generally accepted. It is important to remember that the debate over euthanasia is largely a matter of conscience. People on both sides of the controversy have good intentions; each side can make a compelling moral case for its position.

As difficult as it is for individuals to anticipate or enforce health care choices related to the end of their own lives, the issue becomes even more complex when the choices fall to others.

3

When Others Must Decide

MOST PEOPLE CONCEDE that individuals have the right to refuse or end unwanted medical treatment for themselves. However, when patients are unable to make that choice, others must decide on their behalf. The decision to perform euthanasia—even passive euthanasia—on such a patient raises moral, medical, and legal issues that cannot easily be resolved.

Making decisions for incompetent patients

People who are incapable of understanding explanations and making decisions regarding their own welfare are said to be incompetent. Incompetent patients include those who cannot think clearly or communicate because of injury or illness. Newborn infants with severe and often life-threatening illnesses or birth defects are also included in this group because others must make decisions for them.

Usually relatives or friends act as proxies for incompetent patients. However, sometimes the court appoints a guardian or conservator to fill this role. Proxies arrange for such things as housing, food, clothing, and private nurses. They also meet regularly with the patient's doctors and

(Opposite page) The family of Nancy Beth Cruzan holds a press conference outside the Supreme Court building. Cruzan's family sought the Court's permission to remove her feeding tube and thus decide her fate.

45

make all the important decisions about medical care. Sometimes they must make decisions that may end the patient's life.

A painful decision

In many cases the decision to allow a loved one to die, although painful, is relatively simple. The patient may have prepared a living will or a durable power of attorney at an earlier date to guide family members and physicians. Even when there are no explicit instructions, proxies can often reach a decision based on knowledge of the patient's beliefs and lifestyle.

Jackie Matuseski had to make this decision when her sister Rose suffered several strokes that left her comatose and dependent on life support. Physicians told Jackie that if Rose survived she would probably have extensive brain damage and would lose her legs because of circulatory problems. Jackie and her mother decided to turn off Rose's respirator.

"We didn't want Rose kept on machines and not allowed to die," Jackie says. "Death was a preferable state to any life my sister Rose would have led had she recovered from her coma. I knew my sister wouldn't want to live as a multiple amputee. I knew the likelihood of extensive brain damage."

Hospitals have established procedures for withdrawing or withholding medical treatment from incompetent patients like Rose. Commonly, tests are performed to evaluate the patient's condition and family members meet with the patient's doctors. If the decision is made to end medical treatment, two doctors must sign a statement that there is no possibility the patient will recover. If family members cannot agree among themselves, or if they do not agree with the patient's doctors, most hospitals have an ethics committee to resolve disputes outside of court.

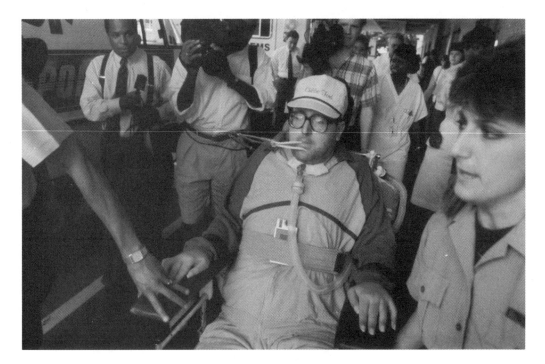

The quality of life possible for an incompetent patient is often an important consideration for families making the decision whether to end or withhold medical treatment. While there is no universally accepted standard for judging quality of life, factors often considered include pain and suffering, mental alertness, the ability to interact with others, helplessness, and the possibility of improvement.

Science writer Isaac Asimov argued eloquently in favor of considering quality of life in such situations. "Are there no conditions when life is meaningless and should be quietly ended?" he asked. "If a person suffers from a disease that deprives him or her of all memory and makes of him or her a helpless lump that may live on for years (in the sense of having the heart and lungs work away automatically and uselessly), must he or she be forced to live on to the slowly prolonged agony and impoverishment of a family?"

After deciding that his life was not worth living, quadriplegic Larry James McAfee successfully fought for the right to disconnect his life-sustaining ventilator.

Opponents of this point of view include anti-euthanasia organizations and groups representing the disabled, who classify withdrawing or withholding medical treatment from incompetent patients as involuntary euthanasia because, they say, the incompetent patient does not have a chance to participate in the decision-making process. They feel it is dangerous to end a life based on an unquantifiable concept like quality of life.

"No one has the right to judge that another's life is not worth living," says a brochure from the Minnesota Citizens Concerned for Life. "The basic right to life should not be revoked because someone decides that someone else's 'quality of life' is too low. Once we base the right to life on 'quality of life' standards, there is no logical place to draw the line."

Concerns about abuse

When an individual holds the power of life and death over another person the possibility of abuse is always a concern. The practice of euthanasia in Nazi Germany in the 1930s resulted in the deaths of more than 100,000 people judged to have no prospect of meaningful life. Nazi officials emptied the country's hospitals of the aged, the handicapped, and chronically ill people of all ages. These patients were shipped off to special institutions to be secretly killed. Later, Nazi officials used this program as a model for the extermination of six million Jews. The experiences of Nazi Germany are a reminder of the potential for grave abuses, especially involving people who cannot speak for themselves.

Substituted judgment

In the United States laws that require proxies to act in the patient's best interest are designed as protection against such abuse. Proxies are al-

Corpses of murdered death camp inmates lie rotting in the sun. Nazi Germany's extermination of millions of Jews and other peoples got its start, in practical terms, in the country's organized euthanasia program.

lowed to make decisions for incompetent patients through a principle called substituted judgment, which the courts identified as valid in the Karen Ann Quinlan case. In that case, the New Jersey Supreme Court reasoned that incompetent people do not lose their rights when they lose their ability to make decisions. Parents or other representatives may exercise those rights (including the right to refuse unwanted medical treatment) on their behalf. However, the decision must reflect the patient's wishes as well as they can be determined.

For nearly two decades, since the Quinlan case, the American legal system has been struggling to define the limits of substituted judgment. The question of just how far the right to refuse medical treatment for someone else extends, and of who should make the final decision, has kept the issue of substituted judgment in the courtroom—and in the headlines. Lately that conflict has focused on tube feeding.

American courts have been inconsistent in deciding whether to allow proxies to end tube feeding. In the 1980s New Jersey, Massachusetts, and California courts expanded substituted decision making to include authorizing the withdrawal of food and fluids. Courts in New York and Missouri have been more cautious, requiring "clear and convincing evidence" of the patient's wishes, such as a living will, before allowing feeding tubes to be withdrawn.

So, in some parts of the United States the family of an incompetent patient whose condition meets accepted guidelines can quietly withdraw the feeding tube and let their loved one die. In others, proxies must petition the court to authorize that act. Sometimes they are successful, sometimes not, but the experience is almost always prolonged and distressing.

Nancy Jobes

One of the first cases to establish family members' right to withdraw tube feeding from an incompetent patient took place in New Jersey. Nancy Jobes became permanently unconscious in 1980 during surgery following an automobile accident. She left no written directive.

Shortly after doctors determined that Jobes was unlikely to improve, her husband, John Jobes III, asked the courts to remove her feeding tube. A superior court judge granted his request in 1986, but the nursing home that cared for Nancy objected. It took the case back to court, saying its policy would not permit starving a patient.

"Starving people to death is so violent, so contrary to our ethic in Western civilization," explained Richard Trainor, an attorney for the facility. "Nancy needs food and water, warmth, clothing and cleanliness. We're obliged to provide those things."

John Jobes told reporters he did not understand the nursing home's vigorous opposition, suggesting it was motivated by the income Jobes generated. "What other reason could they have?" he said. "There's nothing there. Nancy's gone." The nursing home denied any financial motivation for keeping Jobes alive.

The family of Nancy Jobes talks to reporters after hearing the court's 1986 decision allowing them to remove Nancy's feeding tube. When the nursing home caring for Nancy refused to honor the ruling, the family appealed to the New Jersey Supreme Court.

Finally in 1987, seven years after the accident that left Jobes permanently unconscious, the New Jersey State Supreme Court ruled that her family had the right to order the withdrawal of her feeding tube. It commented that most cases like that of Jobes should not even be brought to court. Such decisions, the court said, could be made without legal proceedings by relatives or even close friends of the patient who would "best understand the patient's personal values and beliefs."

Nancy Jobes was moved to another nursing home, where her feeding tube was removed. She died several days later.

Nancy Beth Cruzan

The Missouri Supreme Court reached quite a different decision in a similar case presented at about the same time. Like Nancy Jobes, Nancy Beth Cruzan became permanently unconscious following a car crash. She, too, left no directive. In 1987, four years after her accident, Cruzan's parents sought legal permission to remove her feeding tube. The court would not allow it.

Cruzan's parents lost their first court battle for the right to remove their comatose daughter's feeding tube. The court stated that they failed to establish "clear and convincing evidence" of Nancy's wishes.

"This is not a case in which we are asked to let someone die," the court decision read. "Nancy is not dead. Nor is she terminally ill. This is a case in which we are asked to allow the medical profession to make Nancy die by starvation and dehydration." The document concluded that the elder Cruzans had not shown "clear and convincing evidence," such as a living will, of Cruzan's wishes.

In 1990 new witnesses came forward. Coworkers testified that twelve years earlier Cruzan had told them that she would not want to be kept alive if she were in an irreversible coma. Accepting their testimony, the court finally authorized withdrawing the feeding tube. Nancy Beth Cruzan died December 26, 1990, twelve days after her feeding tube was removed.

Who should have the final say?

When verdicts are contradictory it is difficult to establish standards for the life-and-death decisions that friends and relatives must sometimes make. The AMA's judicial and ethics committee recommends that these decisions remain private, made by family members and the patient's doctor. It suggests that hospital ethics committees step in only when disputes arise.

Derek Humphry, founder of the Hemlock Society, an organization that promotes legalizing voluntary euthanasia, believes that courts should not interfere in the decision-making process unless abuse is suspected. "Nancy's parents should have been left to decide her fate after due consultation with medical staff and anybody else they respected," he commented shortly after Nancy Beth Cruzan's death. "After all, that is what family life is about—supporting (and sometimes even thinking for) relatives so sick they cannot themselves decide."

But David O'Steen, executive director of National Right to Life, an anti-euthanasia organization, and other opponents of euthanasia object to the principle of substituted judgment. He argues that family members should not be entrusted with the sole authority to make choices for incompetent patients because they cannot separate their own biases and interests from those of the patient. O'Steen suggests that an independent authority, such as a medical committee or a judge, review each case to insure that the patient's rights are not abused, that is, not only arbitrate disputes but act as the patient's advocate.

O'Steen's proposal would not allow the family of an incompetent patient to make medical decisions on his or her behalf. It would require the appointment of a legal representative to speak for the incompetent patient and leave the final decision to the official or officials in charge of the hearing.

While this solution leaves open the possibility of euthanasia for an incompetent patient, other proposals would ban it outright. The National Right to Life Committee has drafted model legislation to require continued feeding of incompetent patients except when physicians say they are within hours of death or would suffer unavoidable pain from continuing the procedure. Several states, including Florida, have enacted similar laws.

Letting go

Concerns over the rights of the incompetent patient are especially pronounced when the patient is an infant born with a severe and often life-threatening, but not immediately fatal, condition. In these cases, as in the others, parents and doctors must assess the baby's condition, chances of survival, and quality of life. Decisions are made carefully and usually in private.

This is how it happened for Don and Flora Weber, whose daughter Kimberly was born in 1989 with a severe heart defect that required immediate open-heart surgery. Before doctors could perform the operation, however, a bacterial infection and bleeding that developed inside her skull destroyed most of Kimberly's brain.

The Weber family doctor explained that the outlook was grim. "I told them they had a clear-cut choice," he recalls. "We could operate on the heart and perhaps save her, but she'd be profoundly retarded because the control centers of her brain were destroyed. Or we could let her go."

The Webers decided to forgo the operation. The hospital staff removed life support from the infant. The Webers sat beside their daughter until she died ten days later. "We stayed with her," says Flora Weber. "It was hard to watch our baby die, but we never felt there was any other choice."

Don Weber agrees. "We were upset when it took her so long to die," he says. "We thought it would be over within an hour. Still, our only choice was between maintaining Kimberly on a respirator—where she would have been just a vegetable—and letting her die. We don't feel guilty at all, just sad that we had to lose our little girl."

Don and Flora Weber made the decisions for their daughter without judicial involvement and without controversy. A series of events in the early 1980s challenged the decision-making authority of parents, however, when the decision involves a severely disabled infant.

Baby Doe

On April 9, 1982, a baby boy was born at a small hospital in Bloomington, Indiana. The infant, whose given name was withheld by the courts to protect the identity of his parents, came

to be known as "Baby Doe." Baby Doe was born severely handicapped. He had Down's syndrome, a chromosomal abnormality that includes mental retardation. His throat did not connect properly with his stomach, making it impossible for him to eat or drink. Without surgery this condition would certainly be fatal. Chest X rays also revealed an enlarged heart, another possibly fatal condition.

Mr. and Mrs. Doe consulted with several doctors. Some recommended surgery to correct the stomach abnormality. Dr. Walter Owens, the physician who delivered the baby, urged the Does to reject surgery. He felt it would be kinder to allow the baby to die. Surgery, he said, would cause a great deal of pain and probably have to be repeated several times. He also urged the Does to consider the child's quality of life with Down's syndrome and his other physical ailments. Owens assured the Does that once the feeding tube was removed, the hospital would make the baby's final days as comfortable as possible. After discussing the matter privately, the Does decided against surgery, choosing to let their baby die.

Their decision was challenged in court by the hospital, the county, and by various groups opposed to euthanasia. Two of the hospital's doctors even attempted to kidnap the baby to restart intravenous feeding. By that time, however, it was too late to save Baby Doe.

The federal government steps in

The Baby Doe case attracted national attention. Shortly afterward, the federal government enacted new regulations outlining penalties for withholding food or medical treatment from handicapped infants. On April 30, 1982, just days after Baby Doe's death, the Department of Health and Human Services notified nearly seven thousand American medical institutions that they faced the loss of government financial assistance if they withheld food or medical treatment from handicapped babies.

"It is unlawful," the notice read, "to withhold from a handicapped infant nutritional sustenance or medical or surgical treatment required to correct a life-threatening condition if: (1) the withholding is based on the fact that the infant is handicapped; and (2) the handicap does not render the treatment or nutritional sustenance medically contraindicated [inadvisable]."

Additional regulations were published on March 2, 1983. They required hospitals receiving federal funds to post large warning signs in every

delivery room, maternity ward, and nursery: "DISCRIMINATORY FAILURE TO FEED AND CARE FOR HANDICAPPED INFANTS IN THIS FACILITY IS PROHIBITED BY FEDERAL LAW." The signs gave a hotline number to call to report a handicapped infant being denied food or medical care.

The new regulations effectively took the euthanasia decision out of the hands of doctors and parents by requiring feeding and medical treatment no matter what the baby's condition. The regulations did not withstand the ultimate court test, however.

In April 1983, U.S. district court judge Gerhardt Gesell overturned the Baby Doe regulations. Judge Gesell described them as "hasty and ill-considered." They did little good, he said, except to terrorize doctors and parents into treating every child with birth defects, whether the treatment would be helpful or not. He concluded that the regulations did not take into consideration the possibility that it might be in an infant's best interest to end painful or intrusive treatment when it was clear that the baby was dying.

Later efforts to reinstate the Baby Doe regulations also met defeat in the courtroom although it is no longer considered acceptable to withhold food or treatment from an infant with a nonfatal or correctable condition.

Who should decide?

Doctors, patients, parents, judges, government officials, and political activists all seem to want a say in euthanasia decisions. Yet, for the most part, end-of-life decisions are made just like other medical decisions, by patients, their families, and their doctors. Only a few cases find their way into the headlines. Still, while publicity and court battles may be difficult for individual families to endure, public discussion is beneficial. For, when all sides are allowed to have their say, the rights of the patient receive careful consideration, and society itself begins to reach a clearer understanding of the issues.

U.S. district court judge Gerhardt Gesell overturned health department regulations that required that all handicapped infants be given food and medical treatment regardless of their condition.

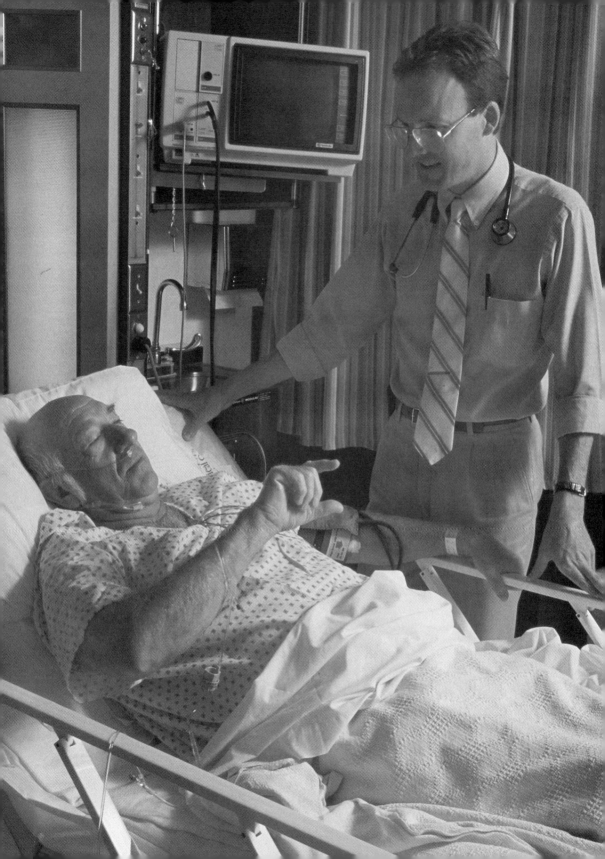

4

Do Doctors Have an Obligation to Help Us Die?

NUMEROUS ADVANCES IN medicine have enabled doctors to keep patients on the verge of death alive for increasingly longer periods of time. However, these same advances have brought with them serious questions about what responsibilities doctors have toward patients who cannot be cured and whose lives are being maintained at the expense of great pain and suffering.

Doctors find themselves at the center of a debate about whether they have the obligation to help these patients end their life. Proposals to allow assisted suicide and other forms of active euthanasia raise issues of ethics, proper medical procedure, and legal responsibility that challenge current views of the practice of medicine and the doctor-patient relationship.

Asking doctors to end life

Physicians are taught in medical school that they have two chief responsibilities: to preserve life and to relieve suffering. For the most part, these responsibilities do not conflict. But when their medical skills cannot restore a patient to

(Opposite page) At the beginning of their careers, doctors promise to help preserve life and relieve suffering. When these responsibilities conflict, as they often do, doctors face difficult decisions.

A protester graphically expresses the view that euthanasia done with a doctor's help is a more humane option than suicide.

health, doctors are sometimes asked to end suffering through a mercifully painless death.

The most common way this happens is that a patient asks his or her doctor to hasten death by prescribing a medication for the patient to take at home. If the doctor agrees, the patient receives a prescription for a pain-relieving drug and instructions on what dosage will be certain to cause death. Far less commonly, a patient who is too incapacitated to take this step for himself or herself will request a lethal injection. Infrequently, patients who depend on respirators or other life-sustaining devices ask their physician to withdraw life support and provide sedatives while they die.

Why should physicians assist suicide?

Since many people are capable of committing suicide without a doctor's assistance, it is reasonable to ask if doctors are obligated to assist someone who wants to die. Supporters of euthanasia give several reasons why physicians ought to provide help to the terminally ill who want to die.

First, those who are terminally ill and wish to commit suicide do not want to suffer. Therefore they want a doctor's help to ensure that their effort to end their life succeeds. They do not want to wake up in the hospital, possibly in a worse condition than before. "You have no idea how depressing it is to try to commit suicide and wake up the next morning to find yourself still alive," said one man who was interviewed for a 1992 Canadian study of suicide among people with AIDS.

Second, sick people often experience difficulty taking medicine and might not be able to swallow an amount of painkillers sufficient to cause death. "It's not easy to die, even if you want to and even if you're terminally ill," says Betty Rollin, an author who has written many articles and several books supporting euthanasia. "A huge number of the right kind of pills will work, but not everyone that sick can swallow, or even move."

Finally, the knowledge that help in dying is available may prevent some desperate terminally ill people from ending their lives prematurely and violently. Ralph Mero, a Unitarian Universalist minister and founder of Compassion in Dying, an organization dedicated to helping patients who wish to hasten their death, says many terminal patients merely need to know they have the option of an early death. He explains that terminal patients sometimes become terrified they will grow too ill too quickly to take their own lives. That fear of being trapped, Reverend Mero says, often pushes them to premature, violent action.

Why physicians should not perform active euthanasia

In spite of the reasons why it might be beneficial for doctors to help some patients end their lives, many doctors feel that performing active euthanasia is contrary to the aims of their profession. This is why the American Medical Association opposes active euthanasia. The organization has published a standard of ethics that bans active euthanasia and physician-assisted suicide because of the possibility of eroding the doctor-patient relationship and the danger of abuse.

An AMA policy statement concludes that there may be circumstances when active euthanasia might seem to be the most humane course of action, "but the . . . risk of involving physicians in medical interventions to cause patients' deaths is too great to [approve of] euthanasia or physician-assisted suicide at this time."

"If you permit physician-assisted suicide, you are giving the medical profession something they

don't want and shouldn't have," sums up A. G. Henderson, lawyer for the Pro-Life and Pacific Physicians groups.

Can doctors assist suicide and still remain healers?

The question at the heart of the debate about assisted suicide is whether doctors can ethically assist suicide and remain healers. Twelve physicians examined this issue in the *New England Journal of Medicine* in 1989. Ten of them agreed that, since doctors are supposed to ease pain and give comfort, it should be an acceptable part of a doctor's role to provide hopelessly ill patients with the knowledge and the means to commit suicide. The group also declared that it should be lawful, under certain circumstances, for physicians to assist patients in ending their lives.

In 1990 a panel of doctors from the British Institute of Medical Ethics reached similar conclusions in a lengthy study of the ethics of prolonging life and assisting death. The doctors wrote in their report:

> In most patients with terminal illnesses, the question of assisting death never arises. Any distressing symptoms are usually relieved by appropriate treatment and patients do not ask for assisted death. But if this relief is not possible, distress is severe, and the patient asks to have his life ended . . . the balance of the moral argument has shifted towards asking why death should not be assisted. The greater the unrelieved pain and distress, the more ethical is a doctor's decision to assist death if the patient desires it.

Over the years, the report says, many doctors have occasionally assisted the deaths of individual patients. These rare acts of euthanasia do not seem to have affected the doctor-patient relationship in a negative way, and have not led to a breakdown in the ethical behavior of physicians. In fact, they have most often been praised as examples of compassion and mercy.

Finally, the report describes the current situation, in which some doctors are willing to provide assistance in dying and others are not, as unfair because some patients may wish to end their lives but be unable to find any physician to help them. Furthermore, since there are no generally accepted medical standards or laws governing the type of euthanasia doctors practice today, the report concludes that abuse is more likely now than it would be if euthanasia were legalized and strictly regulated. Legalizing euthanasia would protect the patient by establishing standards that spelled out when euthanasia was appropriate and how it should be performed. It also would allow doctors to grant sincere requests for help in dying

Sue Rodriquez, a Canadian woman suffering from Lou Gehrig's disease, fought for the right to receive assistance in committing suicide. Two months after the Canadian Supreme Court rejected her bid, Rodriquez ended her life with the help of an unidentified doctor.

without the fear of lawsuits or criminal prosecution.

Why doctors break the law

Doctors who help a patient die despite laws forbidding it say that compassion sometimes overrules other considerations. "It's a kind of situation where your head and your heart are fighting each other," says Dr. George Scott Wallace, a former legislator from Victoria, British Columbia.

In 1993 he told newspapers he would consider helping Sue Rodriquez, a forty-two-year-old Canadian woman suffering from Lou Gehrig's disease, commit suicide. Lou Gehrig's disease is inevitably fatal, but its course can be relatively rapid or unpredictably slow. Sue had been waging a battle in the courts to win the right to assistance in committing suicide.

"Your head tells you that it's against the law, and that it can lead to misunderstanding of a doctor's role in society by doing something that has just legally never been considered before. But anybody that has any kind of heart just has to look at the kind of future that Sue Rodriquez faces and you're bound to feel that someone should show just basic human compassion," Wallace said.

Sue Rodriquez seeks the legal right to assisted suicide

Lawyer Christopher Considine, argued Sue Rodriquez's case before the Canadian Supreme Court. He claimed that the law prohibiting assisted suicide condemned her to suffering inside a body without the ability to move but with a still-active brain. Sue, who came to court in a wheelchair, could commit suicide before she became too incapacitated, her lawyer said, but she wanted the right to die with medical assistance, at a time of her own choosing.

"What Sue Rodriquez is seeking," he told the judges, "is an order from this court which will permit her to control and manage the final stages of her life. Part of that management is to allow her, at the time of her choosing, to end the suffering and indignity and to end the prolonging of her life."

On December 29, 1993, the Canadian Supreme Court rejected Sue Rodriquez's bid to secure the right to assisted suicide, saying that the sanctity of life came before an individual's right to commit suicide. Less than two months later, on February 12, 1994, Sue Rodriquez killed herself with the help of a doctor who has never been identified. Her lawyer released her last statement, which pleaded with Canadian courts to legalize assisted suicide. "I hope my efforts will not be in vain," the statement concluded.

Invisible acts

According to Professor Diane Crane of Johns Hopkins University, most cases of assisted suicide take place in secrecy. When sympathetic doctors help suffering patients end their lives, they do so by providing overdoses of the same painkilling drugs that the patients might normally be prescribed. She calls these cases of euthanasia "invisible acts" because they are secret and virtually undetectable.

Doctors who perform active euthanasia keep it a secret because they face serious consequences. Euthanasia is illegal in all fifty states. In Illinois, Ohio, and Michigan it is considered murder. Doctors suspected of euthanasia are liable to discipline by the AMA, loss of their medical license, and criminal or civil prosecution.

For these reasons it is impossible to say how many doctors hasten patients' deaths through active euthanasia. However, a 1992 survey of four hundred specialists in internal medicine conducted by the American Society of Internal Medicine found that it is relatively common for patients to ask their doctors for help in committing suicide, and that physicians often do take action to hasten death. Almost one-fourth of the doctors surveyed said a terminally ill patient had asked them for assistance in committing suicide. About one-fifth reported that they had deliberately taken steps to cause a patient's death.

Dr. Burns Roehrig, editor of the *Internist*, the journal that published the survey results, cautions that these statistics could be misleading because some doctors might have thought the questions referred to passive euthanasia as well as active euthanasia. However, other surveys have had similar results, including one conducted by *Physician's Management*, which found that one-tenth of American physicians had deliberately ended a patient's life. In another recent survey, about a third of the doctors questioned said active euthanasia is justified in the case of a terminal patient who is in great pain without hope of relief or recovery.

Jack Kevorkian has been dubbed "Dr. Death" for openly assisting in the suicides of numerous people in order to challenge laws against euthanasia.

They call him Dr. Death

Because it is done in secret, and because doctors performing euthanasia are careful to prescribe drugs that are hard to distinguish from routine prescriptions, prosecution of those who have helped a person die is unusual. One exception is Michigan doctor Jack Kevorkian, whom the media has dubbed "Dr. Death."

As a young intern Kevorkian was deeply affected by the first time he saw a severely ill cancer patient. "The patient was a helplessly immobile woman of middle age," he later wrote in *Prescription: Medicide*. "The poor wretch stared up at me . . . as though she was pleading for help and death at the same time. From that moment on, I was sure that doctor-assisted euthanasia and suicide are and always were ethical, no matter what anyone says or thinks."

After a 1986 visit to the Netherlands (where euthanasia is legal under certain circumstances) Kevorkian decided to challenge existing laws against euthanasia in the United States. "I decided to take the risky step of assisting terminal patients in committing suicide," he wrote. "I

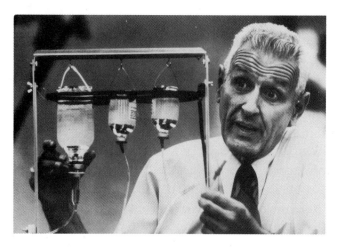

Kevorkian displays his Mercitron, a machine he built to enable terminally ill or severely crippled patients to kill themselves. The machine is activated by a switch, which triggers the release of a lethal dose of drugs through an intravenous tube.

could not even consider performing active euthanasia and . . . being charged with murder in a very hostile [environment]. Merely helping with self-killing would entail less risk. It would also help clarify the law."

The suicide machine

In 1990, using gears from small toys he bought at flea markets, Kevorkian built a suicide machine, a mechanism that could deliver lethal drugs through an intravenous tube when the patient touched a switch. Kevorkian named his creation the Mercitron.

Not long afterwards, the Society for the Right to Die issued a proclamation supporting physician-assisted suicide. Kevorkian responded. He spoke on television and radio, took part in debates, and gave interviews to magazines and newspapers, describing his suicide machine.

After learning about his suicide machine, fifty-four-year-old Janet Adkins contacted him. She was in the early stages of Alzheimer's disease and wanted to avoid the gradual loss of mental faculties characteristic of the illness. On June 4, 1990, in the back of Kevorkian's Volkswagon van, she used the suicide machine to end her life. According to Kevorkian, her last words were, "Thank you, thank you."

Kevorkian was charged with murder in Adkins's death, but because Michigan had no laws against assisting a suicide, all charges were dropped. Stripped of his medical license after Janet Adkins's death, he continued to perform assisted suicides, using carbon monoxide when he could no longer obtain lethal drugs. By early 1993, when a new Michigan law against assisting suicide took effect, Kevorkian had helped fifteen people end their lives. In defiance of the law, he later helped six others die.

Most of the people Kevorkian helped die were middle-aged women suffering from illnesses like cancer, Alzheimer's disease, and multiple sclerosis, a nervous system disease that causes progressive weakness and eventual paralysis. Several of the cases, including Janet Adkins and Marjorie Wantz, provoked controversy because the women were not typical of candidates seeking euthanasia. Janet Adkins was still fit enough to play tennis with her son the day before her suicide. Marjorie Wantz, who had been a patient in a

Janet Adkins is pictured with her husband before her illness. Kevorkian was charged with murder after helping her commit suicide. The charges were later dropped.

Kevorkian appears with Marjorie Wantz on a talk show prior to assisting in her suicide. Wantz's death generated a great deal of controversy because her doctors had been unable to diagnose any specific disease.

mental institution not long before her death, suffered only from a vague problem doctors termed a "pelvic condition" that could not be identified as a specific disease.

Four men committed suicide with the doctor's aid, all in 1993. Most of them suffered from cancer, heart disease, or emphysema, a condition in which the lungs gradually lose their ability to expand and take in air. One case, the assisted suicide of seventy-year-old Hugh Gale, resulted in Kevorkian being accused of murder when investigators turned up a form that indicated that Gale had become anxious and asked for the procedure to be stopped. That case was not prosecuted, but Kevorkian was later charged with violating the new law in three assisted suicides.

Only one of these cases has come to trial. (The other two cases are still pending.) In 1994 the jury found Kevorkian innocent of murdering Thomas Hyde, age thirty, who suffered from advanced Lou Gehrig's disease.

Jury members explained their verdict by saying that the doctor supplied his patient with carbon monoxide in order to spare him further suffering, not to kill him. Shortly after this trial, a Michigan court declared the law against assisted suicide unconstitutional.

Walter Reich, a columnist for the *New York Times*, feels the jury was dishonest in saying that Kevorkian did not intend to kill Thomas Hyde. "Even if the object is to relieve pain and discomfort, the inevitable consequence of gassing someone is to kill him," he points out.

According to the columnist, this decision recognizes killing as a legitimate medical procedure, which might undermine the trust people have in doctors. "The jury has unleashed a process that may well erode the identities of physicians as healers and undermine the trust that all of us must have—especially when we're desperately ill and want to live—that our doctors are agents of life, not death," he concludes.

Reich feels that the jury's decision is the result of the difficulties Americans have in dealing with death. "Society finds terminal illness and terrible suffering a bitter pill to swallow," he explains. "Some physicians, laymen, legislators, jurors, and judges prefer to deal with that pill by sugar-coating it." He suggests that turning the responsibility for ending pain and suffering over to a respected, reassuring figure like a doctor is one way society tries to deal with the unpleasant aspects of death.

A new medical specialty

Kevorkian's activities have been described as dangerous. But Kevorkian does not believe what he is doing is dangerous. He sees himself as challenging outmoded ideas of a doctor's role and bringing merciful release from suffering to patients who desperately need it.

Kevorkian proposes the creation of a new medical specialty called obitiatry. This new specialty would assist terminally ill people in committing suicide, then harvest their organs for use in transplants. Obitiatrists would be specially trained, like psychiatrists. Official suicide centers would allow people to commit suicide in a peaceful setting.

In Kevorkian's scenario, requests for medicide—his term for doctor-assisted suicide—would come from the patient's personal physician. A panel of three obitiatrists would decide whether the patient qualified for euthanasia under previously established guidelines, and two would perform the medicide. If the patient showed any doubt about going through with the suicide, the process would be stopped immediately, and the patient would never be allowed to request medicide again.

Praise and criticism for Kevorkian

Kevorkian's straightforward tactics have brought him both praise and criticism. Dr. Frank A. Oski, director of pediatrics at the Johns Hopkins University School of Medicine, thinks Kevorkian should be praised for exposing the issue of euthanasia to public debate.

> Dr. Jack Kevorkian should be regarded as a hero. He has taken on a tough issue that many physicians have avoided despite the pleas of anguished patients. We have legitimized advance directives, living wills and durable powers of attorney. Aren't we ready for euthanasia?
>
> Dying patients need more than prescriptions for mind-numbing narcotics. They need a personal guide and counselor to assist them on their last journey. . . . The debate has begun, thanks to Dr. Kevorkian. The American public must participate in this debate. After all, it is our lives that are at stake.

However, others—many of them within the euthanasia movement—criticize the crusading doctor. They say some of the people he euthanized, like Janet Adkins and Marjorie Wantz, were not sick enough to be acceptable candidates. Others point out that Kevorkian did not follow his own guidelines for medicide when he continued the euthanasia procedure after Hugh Gale had once halted it.

Moreover, his headline-grabbing tactics have provoked a backlash. Some states with weak laws have made efforts to strengthen them. Derek

Humphry believes this may cause doctors who secretly help terminally ill patients die to stop doing so—or face greater penalties if found out.

A prescription for ethical euthanasia

In response to the furor over Kevorkian's public practice of euthanasia, Timothy Quill and several colleagues have proposed guidelines for physicians who find assisted suicide morally acceptable. First, the patient must, of his or her own accord, clearly and repeatedly request to die rather than continue suffering. Second, the patient's judgment must be clear. Third, the patient must have a condition that is incurable and associated with severe, unrelenting, unbearable suffering. Fourth, the doctor must make sure that the patient's suffering and the request are not the result of inadequate treatment for pain, anxiety, or depression. And last, another doctor who is experienced in treating the pain, anxiety, and depression sometimes felt by the terminally ill should be consulted.

These requirements are intended to insure that the request for euthanasia is voluntary and not the result of depression or mental illness. Patients are to be thoroughly evaluated to make sure that their medical problems would not benefit from further treatment and that their request did not come as a result of depression or anxiety. Finally the procedure would be limited to people who could not be helped by other means, such as continued medical treatments or counseling.

Demanding help in dying

Adoption of standards such as these might have helped Elizabeth Bouvia, who decided to seek help in dying in 1983 at the age of twenty-seven. Bouvia checked into a California hospital and told doctors there she wanted them to help

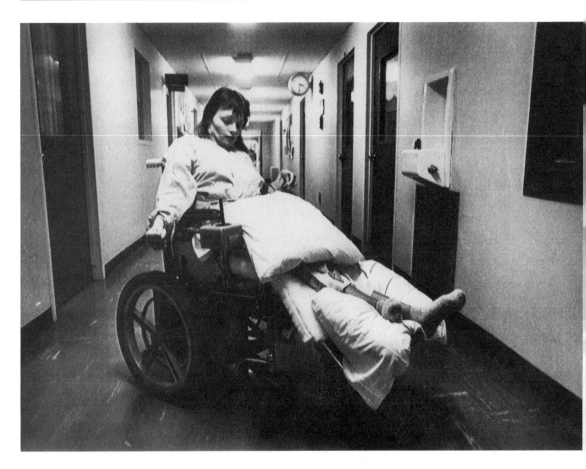

her starve to death. Bouvia, who was almost completely paralyzed by cerebral palsy, asked the medical staff to provide painkillers and basic care while she committed suicide by starvation. She said she wanted to die because of her disabilities.

Bouvia had been paralyzed since birth. Unable to control her arms and legs, she had only limited movement in her right hand and had to be spoon-fed. In 1983 her condition worsened. By the time Bouvia checked into the hospital, she required nursing care twenty-four hours a day and weighed only seventy pounds.

The hospital staff was alarmed by Bouvia's refusal to eat. They inserted a feeding tube against her will and force-fed her. Bouvia hired a lawyer

Paralyzed since birth, Elizabeth Bouvia checked into a hospital and requested that the staff provide painkillers and basic care while she starved herself to death. When the hospital insisted on force-feeding her, Bouvia took her case to court.

and sued the hospital for the right to refuse medical treatment.

She told reporters that she was in constant pain. "It is more of a struggle to live than die. . . . If I really could, I would go out there and kill myself. But I can't. I physically can't." However, Elizabeth agreed to continue to eat until the court decided her case.

Arguments in court

At the court hearing, many groups and individuals presented their own points of view. Representatives of the disabled warned that others would do the same thing if Bouvia's plan were successful. One psychiatrist said Bouvia's desire to kill herself was related to emotional stress. Other specialists said there were times when suicide was a reasonable choice, and that patients like Bouvia had the right to make that choice. Some said that force-feeding violated her right to privacy.

The American Civil Liberties Union provided Bouvia with lawyers, who argued that she had the right to decide privately what type of health care she should receive, as well as the right to be free from unreasonable government intrusion. The hospital's lawyer replied that allowing Elizabeth to refuse medical care was the same thing as helping her commit suicide. "Never can there be a right in a civilized society to tell others, over their moral objections, to assist in a suicide," he told the court.

In late 1983 Judge John J. Hewes ruled: "The court has determined that the ultimate issue is whether or not a severely handicapped, mentally competent person who is otherwise physically healthy and not terminally ill has the right to end her life with the assistance of society. The court concludes that she does not."

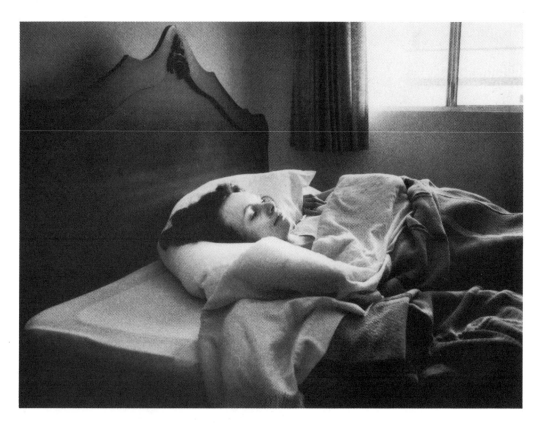

In 1986 this decision was overturned. Bouvia did have a right to refuse the medical treatment that was keeping her alive. But the decision came too late. Side effects of medication she was taking made starvation too painful.

Elizabeth Bouvia has remained hospitalized. She is still helpless. She is still waiting to die. "I've never changed my mind about wanting to die," she told a reporter in the fall of 1992. "I'd rather be dead than live like this."

Although the court granted Bouvia the right to refuse life-sustaining medical treatment, she was unable to follow through with her wish. Side effects of her medication made starvation too painful.

Can we force doctors to help us?

There seems to be no easy answer for people like Elizabeth Bouvia. No one could deny that she was suffering. No one could deny that it was legally allowable for her to refuse unwanted medical treatment. Nevertheless, in many places it *is*

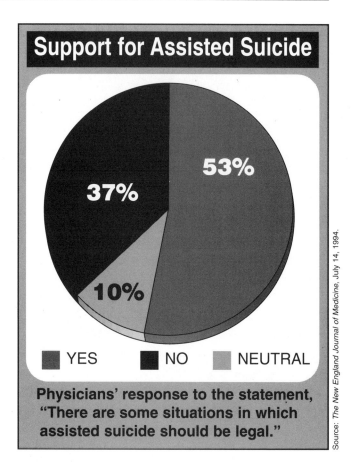

Support for Assisted Suicide

53%

37%

10%

■ YES   ■ NO   ■ NEUTRAL

Physicians' response to the statement, "There are some situations in which assisted suicide should be legal."

illegal to help someone commit suicide, and many health care providers feel it is unethical.

While the California appeals court verdict confirmed Bouvia's rights, it raised many questions about the ethics of asking doctors and hospital workers to honor patients' health care requests. The first question the verdict raised is whether anyone has the right to ask doctors to violate existing laws. Currently there seems to be an unresolved conflict between the right of an individual to make decisions about personal health care and the responsibility of physicians to obey the law. Another question is whether a doctor should be able to refuse a patient's requests because they violate the doctor's professional judgment or personal ethics. The doctors Bouvia wanted help from felt that her case would benefit from further medical treatment, and that helping her die was unethical. The case also asked whether a doctor's obligation to ease suffering and give comfort is limited to procedures that do not cause death. These questions are as yet unresolved.

The controversy continues

Thus, while a broad consensus has emerged in favor of a patient's right to refuse treatment, there is no such agreement on the role that doctors should play in assisting suicide. Doctors themselves are divided on issues of ethics, medical practice, and their legal responsibilities. As long as the influence of medical tradition weighs in on the side opposite to that of the anguish of the terminally ill, the battle over a doctor's rightful role in euthanasia is likely to continue for many years.

5

Legalized Euthanasia

ACTIVE EUTHANASIA IS illegal in most countries of the world. It is condemned by the American Medical Association and most religious bodies. But according to a 1991 public opinion poll conducted by the *Boston Globe* newspaper and the Harvard School of Health, 64 percent—or nearly two out of three Americans—favor some form of active euthanasia for terminally ill patients who request it. Seventy-nine percent of adults under the age of thirty-five support the idea.

In November 1994 Oregon became the first state in the nation to allow doctors to hasten death for the terminally ill. Voters passed a new law known as Measure 18, which authorizes doctors to prescribe a lethal dose of drugs for patients in unbearable suffering who have only six months to live.

The law has two requirements. First, at least two doctors must agree that the patient's condition is terminal. Second, the patient must request the drugs three times, the last time in writing. Patients are expected to take the drugs without a doctor's assistance.

It is too soon to tell how assisted suicide will operate under the new Oregon law. Pro- and anti-

(Opposite page) A majority of Americans are in favor of the legalization of some form of euthanasia. This support has put measures to legalize assisted suicide on the ballot in several states.

euthanasia forces alike say that the best place to look for an example of what the United States would be like if euthanasia were legalized is the Netherlands, where the practice has been allowed for decades. Strictly speaking, euthanasia is not legal in the Netherlands. Euthanasia and assisted suicide are punishable by jail terms of up to twelve years, but doctors are not prosecuted if they follow certain guidelines and notify the coroner of their actions.

Rules passed by the Dutch Parliament in 1993 specify that to be eligible for euthanasia a patient must be mentally competent, suffering unbearable pain, and must repeatedly request assistance in dying. The doctor must demonstrate that his or her conscience allowed no choice but to end the patient's life, and consult a second physician before proceeding.

The Dutch do not make distinctions between doctor-assisted suicide and other forms of euthanasia, as Americans do. In the Netherlands, euthanasia means the active termination of a person's life at his or her request, by a doctor. This, in many cases, takes the form of doctor-assisted suicide.

A 1991 Dutch government study found that euthanasia accounts for between 3 and 6 percent of all deaths in the Netherlands. An additional 35 percent involve medical decisions that are not considered euthanasia, such as removing life support or administering doses of painkillers that may shorten the patient's life.

Of 129,000 deaths in 1990, there were between 4,000 and 6,000 cases of euthanasia. Of these, about one-third happened in hospitals and two-thirds took place at home.

Who performs euthanasia?

Most Dutch euthanasia is performed by family doctors, although today an increasing number of specialists practice it as well. The role of the family doctor is still strong in the Netherlands, unlike the United States. The doctor-patient relationship often endures for many years, and doctors still make house calls. This long-term relationship is the reason most euthanasia cases occur in the patient's home.

The Dutch government survey found that most doctors are willing to perform euthanasia. Nearly 80 percent of Dutch family doctors have deliberately given lethal drugs to terminal patients or assisted in their suicides. Most of the rest say they would help a patient die under certain conditions.

Dr. E. Borst-Ellers, chairperson of the Dutch Health Council, summarizes the feelings of many Dutch physicians. She says, "There are situations in which the best way to heal the patient is to help him die peacefully and the doctor who in such a situation grants the patient's request acts as the healer *par excellence*."

Characteristics of people requesting euthanasia

The survey also revealed that most people requesting euthanasia in the Netherlands are seriously ill, but not always fatally ill. Seventy percent are patients with incurable cancer. Other diseases common in patients requesting euthanasia include Alzheimer's disease, emphysema, and AIDS. People with diabetes, severe arthritis, and multiple sclerosis, diseases not normally considered terminal, also request and receive euthanasia. In about two-thirds of the cases, doctors estimated that the patient had less than two weeks to live when he or she asked to die.

One unexpected result of the survey is the finding that very old people seldom request euthanasia. Researchers conclude that euthanasia is "rare" among those over seventy-five and "very

This young AIDS victim requested assistance in commiting suicide but ended up dying a natural death. AIDS is a common disease among patients who request euthanasia in the Netherlands.

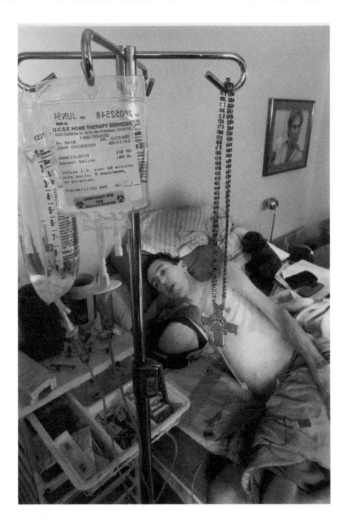

rare" over eighty-five. They speculate that it may be easier for very old people to accept the effects of illness. Another possibility is that older people do not know how to request euthanasia. The average age of those seeking aid in dying is sixty-three for men and sixty-six for women.

The primary reason patients give for requesting aid in dying is unbearable suffering, both physical and psychological. Borst-Ellers points out that this is not merely a question of pain. Patients may experience other symptoms, such as nausea or vomiting, which they find unbearable. Very ill pa-

tients may feel overwhelming psychological pain
due to loss of dignity and the conviction that they
are a burden to their family.

Death by appointment

Typically, euthanasia is arranged by appointment. A Dutch doctor and his or her patient discuss euthanasia for some time before the decision
is reached. They agree that, when the patient decides the time is right, the doctor will help the patient die.

Most patients wait until they feel they are suffering more than they can bear before they set the
date to die. Others will decide in advance, choosing a day of personal importance that is not too
far off, or when family members can conve-
niently be present. In most cases, the euthanasia
takes place within a few days.

Once the decision has been made, the person
who is to die says farewell to distant friends and
family and makes other last-minute arrange-
ments. The patient often has loved ones at hand
when the doctor arrives at the appointed time. After checking once more to be certain that the patient still wants to die, the physician administers a
drug that causes a coma. This may be in the form
of a "cocktail" that the sick person drinks or an
injection given by the doctor if the patient is too
ill to swallow. Then, when the patient is unconscious, an injection of a muscle-paralyzing agent
brings about death.

How doctors feel about euthanasia

Most Dutch doctors find it hard to perform euthanasia. "Doing euthanasia, I'm sick for a week
afterward," says Dr. Hans Wessel, who euthanizes
three or four patients a year. He admits mixed
feelings about it. "Is the patient manipulating me?
Am I playing God?

Dutch doctor Wilifried van Oijen gives a patient suffering from Lou Gehrig's disease a lethal injection. Euthanasia in the Netherlands is typically arranged by appointment.

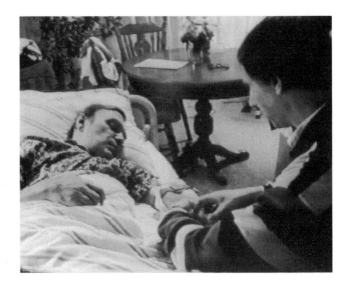

"It's awful to do it, to kill, to execute a life, but it is also a privilege to stand so close to a person, to be so intimate with their feelings and way of life."

Dr. H. S. Cohen, a Dutch general practitioner, argues that allowing euthanasia improves the quality of medical care doctors give. He says Dutch doctors do their best to make life bearable and to find alternatives to euthanasia.

Cohen believes doctors and nurses ought to raise the subject of euthanasia with their patients. When euthanasia is freely discussed, patients know it is available, he says. Then they can accept the end of life with tranquility and even happiness.

Changing rules

In spite of widespread acceptance of euthanasia for the terminally ill in the Netherlands, debate about who has the right to the procedure and how it should be controlled is far from over. The rules limiting euthanasia have been liberalized and, in some cases, disregarded. As a result, doctors in the Netherlands now perform euthanasia on many who at one time would not have been eligible for the procedure. This development has provoked criticism even from supporters of euthanasia.

One criticism is that, contrary to government guidelines, doctors often perform euthanasia on patients who are not mentally competent. One-sixth of all euthanasia cases in the Netherlands reportedly involve severely disabled infants, people in comas, and other incompetent patients.

Dr. Zier Versluys, head of the Dutch Pediatric Association's Working Group on Neonatal Ethics, defends euthanasia as part of good medical practice in the treatment of newborns. "It seems to be automatic that if you see a very sick infant you prolong the life of that infant," the doctor told a reporter for the Associated Press. "But it's not always good to prolong someone's life because life is not always good."

Versluys estimates that euthanasia is practiced about ten times a year on Dutch newborns. "The main problem is that we kept these children alive in the first place," he says. "Both for the parents and the children, an early death is better than life."

Criticism

Another criticism leveled against the Dutch system is that involuntary euthanasia is being performed on incompetent patients—that is, the patient has not requested it. In January 1994 a new law took effect that allows involuntary euthanasia if a doctor can argue that the patient would have wanted it.

Defenders of the law say that it only recognizes the way that responsible doctors have been practicing euthanasia all along. "The new law only formalizes a practice that has been accepted for 20 years," says Johan Legemaate of the Royal Dutch Medical Association. "Doctors do not perform euthanasia for pleasure. They do it to relieve suffering."

A third complaint is that euthanasia is no longer limited to adults. In addition to involuntary euthanasia of defective infants at their parents' request, voluntary euthanasia is performed on teenagers and even younger children, in some cases without their parents' permission. Those who object to this argue that the youngsters have limited understanding of the finality of death.

In 1992 a committee of the Royal Dutch Medical Association studying who receives euthanasia and how the decision is made recommended that children should be allowed to obtain euthanasia, even if their parents object. Committee members felt that severely ill youngsters are often capable of evaluating their own condition and making decisions for themselves, while grief or guilt sometimes keeps parents from admitting that their child would be better off dead.

"Sometimes a 15-year-old child can have mature judgment," the committee's report said, "and sometimes parents can have immature judgment."

Finally, even the requirement that the person receiving euthanasia be in "unrelenting physical pain" has been relaxed. In 1994 the Dutch

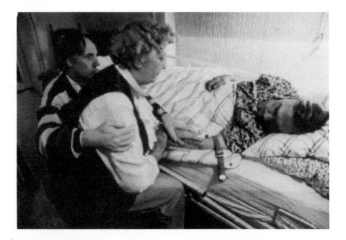

Van Oijen comforts his patient's wife while the injection takes effect. Euthanasia in the Netherlands is not illegal provided that doctors follow rules set forth by the Dutch Parliament governing its practice.

Supreme Court ruled that a patient need not be in severe pain to receive euthanasia. A woman named Hilly Bosscher convinced her psychiatrist to provide her with the drugs to commit suicide. Bosscher told the doctor that a failed marriage and the deaths of her two sons had caused her to lose the will to live.

The court found the psychiatrist, Dr. Boudewijn Chabot, guilty of violating government guidelines and performing euthanasia in a case where the patient was not suffering severe pain. However, Chabot was not punished because the members of the court felt that he had acted out of compassion for the woman's emotional suffering. This ruling is expected to establish mental suffering as an acceptable reason for euthanasia in the Netherlands.

Is abuse inevitable?

Opponents of euthanasia see this relaxing of the rules limiting euthanasia in the Netherlands as evidence that abuse will inevitably take place. Susan Wolfe, a lawyer and researcher at the Hastings Center in New York, who opposes active euthanasia in any form, sums up these feelings when she says, "The practice of euthanasia is seeping beyond the guidelines that are meant to confine it. . . . Evidently the process is not workable. We have yet to see a process that *is* workable."

Thomas Murray, an ethicist at Case Western Reserve University who supports assisted suicide in certain cases, also has reservations about how the Dutch system is working. "There is some evidence that doctors are deciding on behalf of patients when it is time for them to go," he says. "That's always what people who have qualms about active euthanasia and assisted suicide worry about."

"Ethics won't allow us to pull the plug until he runs out of money."

He opposes legalizing euthanasia in the United States for the same reason. "[It's] not because I think people always are morally wrong when they do it, but because I fear that, once legalized, it would become so open for errors as well as potential abuses."

But not everyone draws such a direct parallel between euthanasia in the Netherlands and euthanasia in the United States. Teresa A. Takken, a Dutch woman who is both an ethicist and a Roman Catholic nun, says she considers abuse of euthanasia in the Netherlands unlikely. Sister Takken explains that the Dutch system of welfare and free medical care keep the poor and elderly from worrying about the high cost of medical care, a consideration that might make them seek euthanasia. Moreover, Dutch doctors know their patients on an individual basis, and spend a great deal of time with someone who asks for help ending his or her life, trying to make certain that this is truly the patient's wish. These characteristics of the Dutch medical system prevent abuse and keep requests for euthanasia at a minimum.

However, Sister Takken contends abuse *could* occur in countries like the United States, where health care is expensive and doctors do not have such close personal relationships with their patients. Sick people might turn to euthanasia after finding themselves unable to work and faced with mounting medical expenses, and doctors who do not know them well might not take the time to find out the real reason behind their request. "We have no business even talking about euthanasia here [in the United States] until we have health care for all," she says.

Dr. Peter McGough, a family practitioner in the state of Washington, supports this point of view. He believes that the fear of burdening their families financially would lead many underprivileged Americans to seek a doctor's assistance in dying if it were available. According to McGough, the poor, the underinsured and the uninsured are

Washington family practitioner Peter McGough believes that euthanasia should not be legalized in the United States until health care is available for all.

particularly afraid of death, since they have limited access to health care and sometimes no way to pay for it.

"People have very real fears about end-of-life care," he says. "They would choose to end their lives with a physician's help rather than place any financial burden on their families. This is a sad reflection on our health-care system."

The euthanasia movement in the United States

While opponents of euthanasia are concerned with the possibility of abuse, supporters talk about the pain and suffering that allowing doctors to perform active euthanasia will spare dying people. Michael H. White, a California lawyer who in 1992 sponsored a proposed law allowing doctors to help terminally ill patients kill themselves, claims doctors owe a merciful death to their patients. "If a physician can't deal with pain and suffering, there ought to be a right for the patient to ask for compassionate aid-in-dying."

Two organizations, the Hemlock Society and Compassion in Dying, are trying to secure the right to active euthanasia in the United States. In 1980 Derek Humphry founded the Hemlock Society, named for the poison the Greek philosopher Socrates drank when ordered to commit suicide. The group, which has more than fifty thousand members, campaigns for the right of terminally ill patients to die with the help of a doctor if possible. Compassion in Dying is a newer group, begun in 1993 to actively help terminally ill people commit suicide and to lobby for legalized euthanasia.

Like others in the euthanasia movement, Derek Humphry became an activist because of personal experience. He says he helped his first wife commit suicide when breast cancer made her life unbearable, and he has written a book called *Final Exit* that gives suicide advice.

In 1980 Derek Humphry founded the Hemlock Society, an organization that campaigns for the right of the terminally ill to request both active and passive euthanasia.

The Hemlock Society supports both active and passive euthanasia for terminally ill people who request it. However, Humphry says, "I think once it was decided by doctors and family and all concerned that a person should be starved to death [by the withdrawal of nutrients and fluids], I think it would be more honest and humane to . . . give them an injection and end their life [by active euthanasia, rather] than wait, say 20 days while they die."

Compassion in Dying is an organization dedicated to helping patients who wish to "hasten their dying" and to show that rules can be set up for assisted suicide which protect vulnerable people. Leaders of the group have developed a set of strict guidelines they hope to see made into law someday.

The organization will only help adults who are terminally ill, mentally competent, and would not require assistance in taking lethal drugs if they were made available to them. Patients must have the support of both their personal doctor and their families and must not be acting out of depression, financial worries, or because they lack adequate emotional support or medical care.

Applicants for assistance are evaluated by representatives of Compassion in Dying according to these guidelines. Those who qualify receive information on lethal doses of drugs, family counseling, and even the support and comfort of a trained volunteer if they decide to take their own lives.

Legalizing aid in dying

Since 1988, the Hemlock Society, the Society for the Right to Die, Americans Against Human Suffering, and other groups have campaigned to put physician-assisted death on the ballot in several states. In 1991 the state of Washington was the first to vote on the issue. Initiative 119, known as the Death with Dignity initiative, proposed making it legal for a doctor to give dying patients who request it a lethal injection or a lethal dose of drugs to take themselves. Under Initiative 119, candidates for aid in dying would be terminally ill or have an irreversible condition that, in the opinion of two physicians, would result in death within six months.

Early public opinion polls favored the measure by a 2 to 1 margin. Numerous liberal religious groups supported it, as well as nearly half the state's physicians. Still, Initiative 119 was defeated, following a last-minute advertising campaign against it. Political analysts felt that the uproar over Jack Kevorkian and his controversial cases of assisted suicide contributed to the defeat.

The following year, a similar proposition appeared on the California ballot. Proposition 161, known as the Humane and Dignified Death Act, contained provisions similar to those in Initiative 119, with added safeguards. The request for aid in dying must be signed by a competent adult and two impartial witnesses. A patient who is weak, feeble, or incompetent cannot receive aid in dying unless the request was made earlier, when the patient was still mentally sound. And a patient may revoke the request at any time. Finally, hospitals and other health care facilities where patients received aid in dying must keep careful records.

This measure failed, too. But out of nearly ten million votes cast, more than four and a half million were in favor of the proposition. In 1994 Jack Kevorkian failed to gather enough signatures to put his initiative for legalizing euthanasia on the Michigan ballot. Analysts theorize that these measures failed because they would have allowed doctors to administer lethal drugs to their patients.

Oregon's assisted-suicide law differs from earlier proposals. Doctors are allowed to prescribe a lethal dose of drugs, but cannot administer it. In spite of this difference, many experts believe that the bill will open the door to legalizing assisted suicide in other states. "It's just the first domino to fall," says Geoffrey Fieger, attorney and spokesman for Kevorkian.

"The legalization of any form of assisted suicide will have just tremendous consequences that will reverberate through American society," says Arthur Caplan, director of the Center for Bioethics at the University of Pennsylvania School of Medicine in Philadelphia.

Supporters of euthanasia in other states say they will continue to try to enact assisted-suicide bills. California, Washington, Florida, Arizona, and Michigan seem the likeliest to find aid-in-dying measures on the ballot in the near future.

Losing at the polls, winning in the courts

In the meantime, euthanasia supporters have found success in court. After Washington State refused to make assisted suicide legal in 1991, Compassion in Dying took the issue to court, eventually winning its case in the spring of 1994.

U.S. district court judge Barbara Rothstein became the first federal judge to rule that terminally ill people have a constitutionally guaranteed right to end their lives. In her decision Judge Rothstein said that the right to suicide is protected by the right to decide what to do with one's own body, the same right that guided the Supreme Court's legalization of abortion. The judge also concluded that a right to assisted suicide—or active euthanasia—is identical to the right of patients, already recognized by courts, to refuse unwanted medical treatment. Legal experts caution that the decision is likely to be appealed.

Kevorkian's challenge to the new Michigan law against assisted suicide is likely to wind up in the U.S. Supreme Court as well. While one court declared the law unconstitutional, the Michigan Supreme Court has stated that there is no constitutional right to assisted suicide.

Inching toward legalization

To many observers, the United States seems to be inching towards legalization of at least some types of active euthanasia. Aggressive campaigns to win voter approval of doctor-assisted suicide initiatives have already come very close to succeeding, and now the federal courts seem likely to recognize assistance in dying as a right.

If doctor-assisted suicide or some other form of active euthanasia becomes legal in the United States, an unknown number of people are likely to seek this type of death as an end to their suffering. According to Derek Humphry, founder of the Hemlock Society, the number will be small. "[Doctor-assisted suicide] is not going to happen all the time," he says. "Nobody wants to die. It's for those who want it, deserve it."

He points out that many support the principle of euthanasia who might not take the option if it were available. For example, he says, only 5 percent of the Hemlock Society's membership is terminally ill. The remaining 95 percent is made up of healthy people who want to be able to choose assisted suicide if they feel they need it later on.

Experts in suicide like Dr. Yeats Conwell say that few terminal patients would be likely to choose euthanasia. Conwell says that dying patients seldom want to kill themselves. In a study of forty-four dying cancer patients he found that only three had considered suicide, and each of them had been diagnosed as clinically depressed.

Dr. David Clark, another suicidologist, agrees. He reports that the terminally ill are only slightly

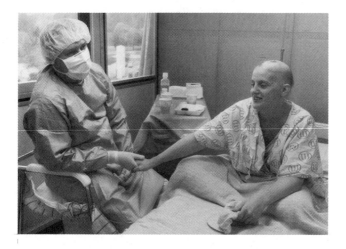

Despite the suffering and depression common among cancer patients, few actually choose suicide.

more likely than other Americans to commit suicide. Those with terminal illnesses make up 1.4 percent of the population and only 2 to 4 percent of suicides.

It is uncertain what forms legalized euthanasia would take in the United States. Jack Kervorkian says he wants every city to have public euthanasia centers. Other euthanasia advocates believe that doctor-assisted suicide in America should follow the Dutch pattern: quiet and personal, a private decision made between patients, their doctors, and their families. The future of euthanasia in America will be determined in part by the public and its needs, and in part by proposals still being formulated by those on both sides of the euthanasia debate.

6

Searching for Answers

IT IS DIFFICULT to determine how often all the different kinds of euthanasia take place. Euthanasia that is both voluntary and passive occurs every day in hospitals and nursing homes across the country. Doctors, patients, and their families decide privately what is the best course of action at the end of life. Perhaps as many as one of every ten deaths involves the decision to end or refuse life-sustaining medical treatment. By all accounts, true active euthanasia is far rarer, happening no more than once or twice in a doctor's career.

No one knows for certain whether this situation would change if euthanasia became legal, but the moral, medical, and legal consequences would be great. Doctors and their patients, as well as experts on ethics and law, are searching for answers to the issues.

Moral solutions

There can be no single correct answer for everyone to the question of euthanasia. Just as each human being is an individual, each death is unique. However, the debate over the morality of euthanasia does seem to be heading towards agreement on certain issues.

(Opposite page) A hospital patient tries to come to terms with her illness. Euthanasia is usually a private matter, decided by doctors, patients, and their families.

101

There is a growing consensus that competent patients should be permitted to weigh the benefits and burdens of alternative treatments—including the alternative of no treatment—according to the patient's values and to refuse any treatment or select from among available treatments.

Another area of agreement is that similar values should be applied to decision making on behalf of incompetent patients. Recent court cases have allowed guardians to remove respirators from permanently unconscious patients and discontinue treatment of babies who are clearly dying. In other cases, the removal of fluids and nutrition supplied by feeding tubes has become an accepted fact. However, doctors and family members must follow established guidelines that tell them when it is appropriate to end medical treatment intended to cure or to maintain life, and what types of supportive treatment, such as pain medication, ought to be continued.

Doctor-assisted suicide

Another area of liberalization is the growing feeling that it is as ethical for a doctor to perform

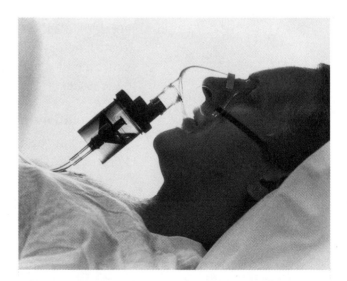

Recent court cases have given guardians the right to remove respirators, feeding tubes, and other medical appartuses that sustain life when a patient has no chance for recovery.

active euthanasia as it is to perform passive euthanasia. More doctors are considering the circumstances under which they would help a patient die. Timothy Quill and several associates published guidelines for physicians administering euthanasia in the *New England Journal of Medicine* in 1991.

A national poll conducted jointly by Harvard University and the *Boston Globe* newspaper in 1991 found widespread public support for the point of view that doctors should be involved if a terminally ill person decides to end his or her life. Sixty-four percent of those surveyed supported the idea of doctor-assisted suicide and euthanasia for terminally ill patients who request it. Additionally, 17 percent of those who agreed with doctor-assisted suicide even thought doctors should be *required* to give lethal injections if the patient asks.

Only 30 percent of all those surveyed said doctor-assisted suicide should be forbidden. While most felt terminally ill patients ought to have the option of assisted suicide, only about half said they would request it for themselves.

Interestingly, most of the Americans polled felt that euthanasia should not be performed by someone outside the medical profession. Only 37 percent agreed that relatives or friends should be allowed to help a terminally ill person end his or her life. Moreover, few would help a loved one die. Only 14 percent said they would assist a terminally ill friend or relative in committing suicide.

A cry from the heart

Leading authorities do not agree on how to interpret the poll. Philosopher Margaret Battin of the University of Utah thinks the poll reflects Americans' fear that doctors and hospitals will

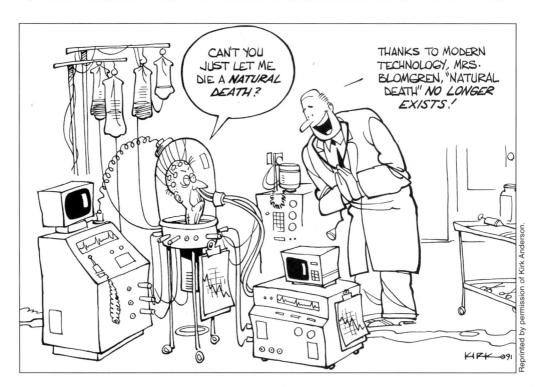

control them at the end of life. She sees the results as the public's protest against the way it believes the medical establishment treats dying patients.

"I think it's really an issue of control," she says. "Who is going to have control? The person who is dying or the person who is caring for the one who is dying?"

Dr. Marcia Angell, editor of the *New England Journal of Medicine*, thinks the prospect of being trapped by modern medical technology frightens many Americans. "People are trying to tell us something," she says. "There's a great perception out there that high-tech medicine has gotten out of hand and is causing a lot of suffering at the end of life. We're hearing a cry from the heart."

Writers at the *Boston Globe* feel their poll reflects widespread sympathy for patients who choose to kill themselves when faced with long, painful illnesses. They think the fear of unwillingly being kept alive by doctors and hospitals also helps explain the rising suicide rate among the elderly and the success of the suicide guide *Final Exit.*

The dying want control and comfort

For many people, euthanasia is a way of maintaining control over their lives. Advocates of legalized euthanasia sometimes present it as a kind of insurance policy against being forced to endure a prolonged and painful dying process. Jackie Matuseski, who had to decide whether to remove her comatose sister Rose from life support, sums up this point of view by saying, "Every day we make decisions about living. Why should it be any different in our dying?"

Reverend Ronal Mudd, hospital chaplain at Methodist Hospice of Jacksonville, Florida, testified before Congress about the needs of terminally ill patients. He says dying patients want to feel that they are still in control of their lives, and that they are still important human beings.

"Terminally ill patients want to have dignity and identity, and some kind of control over their living and dying," he says. "They want to be treated as a person and not as a number, a case, or an object. Many patients want as much control over their destiny in dying as in living." Patients also want to be as free of pain as possible "without being drugged out of their minds," he adds.

Controlling pain

According to the Public Health Service Agency, most people imagine that the end of life will be filled by uncontrollable pain, and they fear it. Some authorities see this fear as the major factor behind Amercians' support for legalized euthanasia.

The fear of having no ability to prevent a slow, agonizing death prompts many healthy people to support the legalization of assisted suicide.

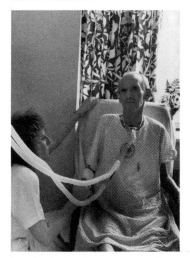

Professor George Annas of Boston University supports this point of view. He considers the Harvard/*Boston Globe* survey results a condemnation of the medical profession. According to Annas, the failure of doctors to provide adequate pain control at the end of life will force Americans to demand euthanasia as an alternative to a painful death. "Unless physicians begin to respond more humanely with pain medication at the end of life," he says, "public calls for legalizing medical assistance in death will inevitably increase and ultimately prevail."

Doctors can do much more to ease severe pain. In a survey of twelve hundred cancer specialists conducted by the Public Health Service Agency, 50 percent admitted they are not doing an adequate job of controlling cancer pain. They estimated that 85 percent of their cancer patients do not receive enough pain medication. These results agree with earlier studies that found 50 to 70 percent of American cancer patients are undermedicated for pain.

Why allow patients to suffer?

According to the Public Health Service Agency, physicians do not give enough pain medication because they accept old myths about pain control. First, they are afraid patients will become addicted. This fear has been increased by recent criticism in America of doctors who prescribe too many pain medications, although none of the controversial cases involved patients with terminal illnesses. Doctors also believe pain is an inescapable part of being ill. Finally, they continue to accept outmoded ideas about the needs of their patients. They may think old people do not require as much medication, or babies do not feel pain.

All of these beliefs are false. For example, only one in twelve thousand patients becomes addicted

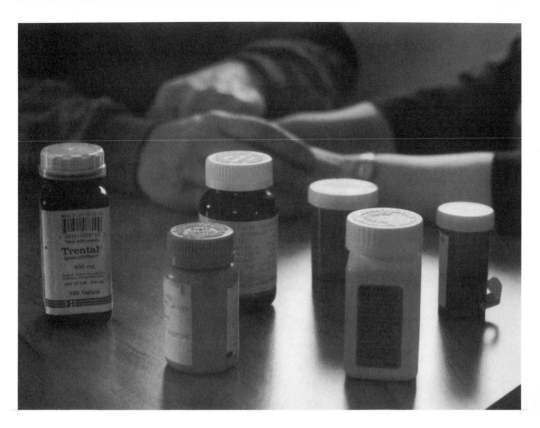

to painkillers. And even these rare cases can usually be easily weaned from the drugs.

The Public Health Service Agency has recently released new guidelines on the use of painkilling medicine. Experts in pain relief expect the guidelines to help educate American doctors about pain control. However, most agree with Dr. John Loeser, chief of the pain center at the University of Washington, who calls for better training and improved standards of pain relief in hospitals.

"We need to dramatically improve pain management education in medical schools, where there is virtually none, and in nursing schools," he says. "We need quality-assurance standards in hospitals that include assessing the adequacy of pain management. Doctors should not get away with not treating pain."

Painkillers can play an important role in relieving suffering. Contrary to what many doctors believe, few patients become addicted to painkillers.

The fact that so many patients undergo unnecessary suffering is especially shocking considering how easy it is to treat pain. Cancer, which now accounts for about 20 percent of American deaths, does involve severe pain in about half the cases. However, 95 percent of the patients in hospices (where cancer is the major diagnosis and painkilling drugs are readily available) report excellent to complete pain relief.

The World Health Organization concludes that "a handful of [simple] drugs can control 80 to 90 percent of cancer pain." Dr. Ronald Dubner, a pioneer in pain research, agrees. "Almost all acute pain and cancer pain can be eliminated or reduced to levels that patients can tolerate," he says.

Hospice care

An alternative to euthanasia that stresses pain management can be found in the hospice movement. In hospice care, a team of trained doctors, nurses, counselors, therapists, and volunteers provides medical care and support not only to the terminally ill patient, but to the whole family. Hospice care in patients' homes, in hospitals, or in separate hospice facilities provides dying patients humane and compassionate care that focuses on easing suffering, rather than curative treatment or hastening death. Up-to-date methods of pain and symptom control allow the patient to live as fully and comfortably as possible.

The typical hospice patient has a life expectancy of six months or less. Most receive care at home. While hospice care is not for everyone, it is grounded in traditional medical principles of giving comfort to the dying, rather than helping them end their lives. Many dying patients find that it enables them to make the most of the remainder of their lives.

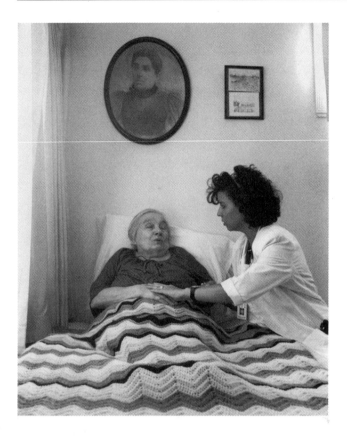

Hospice caregivers provide pain control and emotional support to terminally ill patients, allowing them to live the remainder of their lives as comfortably and fully as possible.

Whether the issue is the right to die, the rights of incompetent patients, doctor-assisted suicide, or any of the other controversial aspects of the euthanasia debate, one thing is certain. The subject of euthanasia is a complex and emotional one.

Each of us has personal feelings and beliefs about the value of life, which may conflict with those of others. For some, allowing or helping someone to die is morally unacceptable. For others, letting a loved one suffer is equally wrong. Doctors and their patients, lawmakers and judges are gradually finding their way through their differences to a national consensus that will respect the rights of the individual while protecting the helpless.

Appendix I

Euthanasia Around the World

Here is an overview of euthanasia and physician-assisted suicide and the laws governing them in eleven countries around the globe.

Canada punishes euthanasia and assisted suicide by a sentence of fourteen years in prison.

France treats euthanasia as homicide. However, some French doctors specialize in "helping the patient to die," the double-effect procedure that aims at easing suffering but not deliberately causing death.

Germany does not use the term *euthanasia* because of its connection with the Nazi era. Instead, Germans speak of "death help." Euthanasia and physician-assisted suicide are punishable by up to five years in jail. However, in most instances people convicted of practicing euthanasia receive suspended sentences or pay a fine.

Great Britain treats euthanasia and physician-assisted suicide as homicide. Both pro- and anti-euthanasia groups are active. Unofficial sources estimate that thousands of cases of euthanasia go unreported.

Israel bans euthanasia. In practice, however, doctors are allowed to follow a patient's instructions not to prolong life by artificial means.

Italy considers euthanasia murder. However, authorities usually take the circumstances of the mercy killing into account and hand out light sentences. There is a developing pro-euthanasia movement, but no legislative action has yet been proposed.

Japan has no official guidelines. Regional courts make the decision whether to punish cases of euthanasia. In 1962 the Nagoya court set a precedent by allowing euthanasia if it is performed by a doctor.

Mexico considers euthanasia murder. However, no laws deal specifically with euthanasia. There have been no cases reported in Mexico, where most of the population is Roman Catholic.

The Netherlands has legalized voluntary euthanasia. Most cases are assisted suicides performed by the patient's private physician, who must consult with another physician before the act.

South Africa classifies euthanasia and physician-assisted suicide as murder. However, courts take the circumstances of mercy killings into consideration. A doctor who killed his terminally ill father in 1975 received only a suspended sentence. He was allowed to resume medical practice two years later.

The United States considers euthanasia a crime—usually murder or manslaughter. Unsuccessful attempts to legalize euthanasia date back to the 1930s. More recently, voters in Washington and California defeated bills to legalize mercy killing. In the meantime, Dr. Jack Kevorkian has inspired controversy by overtly helping more than twenty people kill themselves since 1990.

Appendix II

A Sample Living Will
California Declaration*

If I should have an incurable and irreversible condition that has been diagnosed by two physicians and that will result in my death within a relatively short time without the administration of life-sustaining treatment or has produced an irreversible coma or persistent vegetative state, and I am no longer able to make decisions regarding my medical treatment, I direct my attending physician, pursuant to the Natural Death Act of California, to withhold or withdraw treatment, including artificially administered nutrition and hydration, that only prolongs the process of dying or the irreversible coma or persistent vegetative state and is not necessary for my comfort or to alleviate pain.

If I have been diagnosed as pregnant, and that diagnosis is known to my physician, this declaration shall have no force or effect during my pregnancy.

Other instructions:

Signed this _____ day of _____ , _____
Signature_____
Address_____

The declarant voluntarily signed this writing in my presence. I am not a health care provider, an employee of a health care provider, the operator of a community care facility, an employee of an operator of a community care facility, the operator of a residential care facility for the elderly, or an employee of an operator of a residential care facility for the elderly.

Witness _____

Address _____

The declarant voluntarily signed this writing in my presence. I am not entitled to any portion of the estate of the declarant upon his or her death under any will or codicil thereto of the declarant now existing or by operation of law. I am not a health care provider, an employee of a health care provider, the operator of a community care facility, an employee of an operator of a community care facility, the operator of a residential care facility for the elderly, or an employee of a residential care facility for the elderly.

Witness _____

Signature _____

This directive complies in form with the Natural Death Act, California Health and Safety Code, Section 9188.

*(Revised 1991)

Glossary

active euthanasia: Mercy killing by direct action, such as administering lethal drugs.

advance directive: A legal document that gives instructions about the kind of medical care the signer wishes if he or she is incapable of making those decisions.

Alzheimer's disease: A progressive disease of the brain that destroys the patient's memory and reasoning ability, and results in death.

assisted suicide: Someone (usually a doctor, relative, or close friend) provides the patient with the means and knowledge to take his or her own life; the patient performs the life-ending act under that person's guidance.

best interest: The legal principle that requires decisions made by parents or other guardians to be based on what is best for the incompetent person.

brain stem: The lower part of the brain, which controls automatic body functions, such as breathing and heartbeat. Mechanical support can maintain a heartbeat only temporarily when the brain stem is no longer functioning.

cardiopulmonary: Having to do with the heart and lungs.

competency: A reflection of the ability of persons to make decisions for themselves; those who can make their own decisions and express them are described as competent while someone in a permanently unconscious state would be considered incompetent.

contagious: Spread from person to person by contact.

controversy: Subject that arouses debate or opposing opinions.

degenerative: Causing a gradual loss of vitality and ability to function.

dehydration: Severe lack of fluids, which if untreated can lead to death.

DNR: Stands for do not resuscitate, a code put in the files of hospital patients that authorizes medical workers not to revive them from cardiac or respiratory failure.

durable power of attorney: A document that authorizes another person (usually not a doctor) to make medical decisions for the signer if he or she is unable to do so.

ethics: The study of morality and standards of behavior.

euthanasia: Causing or aiding in death, to end suffering.

hospice: A program of treatment for dying patients that aims to keep them comfortable, rather than to cure them.

informed consent: The legal principle that patients must know, understand, and agree to any medical treatment they receive.

intravenous: Providing nutrition, fluids, or medication directly into the bloodstream.

involuntary euthanasia: Mercy killing administered without the recipient's consent; for example, to babies or incompetent adults.

irreversible: Permanent.

living will: A legal document instructing a physician to withhold or withdraw medical treatment from its signer if he or she is in a terminal condition and unable to make decisions about medical treatment.

passive euthanasia: Withholding or withdrawing means of maintaining or prolonging life; for example, removing a respirator from a person who cannot breathe without assistance.

permanently unconscious state: A continuing condition in which the patient has no awareness.

prolong: To extend or lengthen the time it takes for something to happen.

proxy: Someone who acts on behalf of another person in legal matters.

respirator: A device that provides air to the lungs of patients who cannot breathe on their own.

resuscitate: To revive or bring back to life.

substituted judgment: The legal procedure of allowing a family member or other guardian to make decisions for an incompetent patient, if they base their decision on the patient's point of view.

suicide: The act of killing oneself.

terminal illness: An incurable or irreversible condition that will cause death in a relatively short time. Some state courts are expanding the term to include a condition in which death will occur if treatment, including supplying nutrition and fluids, is removed.

tube feeding: Supplying nutrients and liquids to a patient through a tube inserted into the nose, stomach, or vein.

voluntary euthanasia: Mercy killing administered to one who asks for it.

Organizations
to Contact

The following organizations are concerned with the issues covered in this book. All of them have publications or information available for interested readers.

American Life League (ALL)
P O Box 1350
Stafford, VA 22555
(703) 659-4171

The American Life League is a service organization that provides educational materials, books, flyers, and programs for local, state, and national right-to-life organizations. Among its divisions is the Teen American Life League.

American Medical Association (AMA)
515 State St.
Chicago, IL 60610
(312) 464-4818

Founded in 1847, the American Medical Association has more than 270,000 members. It informs member physicians on important medical and health legislation and represents the medical profession before Congress and governmental agencies. The AMA sets standards for medical schools, hospitals, doctor training programs, and continuing medical education courses.

Americans United for Life (AUL)
343 S. Dearborn St., Suite 1804
Chicago, IL 60604
(312) 786-9494

Americans United for Life is a legal and educational organization concerned with protecting human life at all stages of development. It provides expert testimony, model legislation, and legal briefs in cases involving euthanasia or abortion.

Association for Retarded Citizens of the United States (The ARC)
500 E. Border St., Suite 300
Arlington, TX 76005
(817) 834-7700

The ARC is a national association of parents, professional workers, and others interested in individuals with mental retardation. It works on local, state, and national levels to promote services, research, and public understanding for mentally retarded persons and their families.

Center for the Rights of the Terminally Ill
P O Box 54246
Hurst, TX 76054-2064
(817) 656-5143

The Center for the Rights of the Terminally Ill represents patients, students, physicians, nurses, attorneys, anti-euthanasia organizations, and disability rights groups that seek to ensure competent, professional, compassionate, and ethical health care for the elderly, the handicapped, and the sick and dying. It opposes euthanasia and assisted suicide. The center distributes information on euthanasia and related subjects.

Choice in Dying
200 Vaak St.
New York, NY 10014
(212) 366-5540

Choice in Dying was formed in 1992 by a merger of the Society for the Right to Die, established in 1938, and Concern for Dying, established in 1967. Its goal is to educate the public on the legal, ethical, and psychological implications of terminal care decision making. Choice in Dying distributes copies of the living will.

The Hastings Center
255 Elm Rd.
Briarcliff Manor, NY 10510
(914) 762-8500

The Hastings Center conducts research on issues of medical ethics. Members include doctors, nurses, lawyers, medical administrators, public policy makers, and other academic and health care professionals. It publishes the *Hastings Center Report*.

Hemlock Society
P O Box 11830
Eugene, OR 97440-4030
(503) 342-5748

The Hemlock Society supports the option of active voluntary euthanasia for people who are in the last stages of a terminal illness or who suffer from a serious incurable illness. Members believe that the final decision to end one's life should be one's own. The society publishes the *Hemlock Quarterly*, as well as numerous books and source materials on legal, medical, and social aspects of the right-to-die movement.

Human Life International
7845-E Airpark Rd.
Gaithersburg, MD 20879
(301) 670-7884

Human Life International serves as a research, educational, and service program offering positive alternatives to what the group calls the antilife, antifamily movement. It provides research on euthanasia and infanticide, among other topics.

International Anti-Euthanasia Task Force (IAETF)
P O Box 760
Steubenville, OH 43952
(614) 282-3810

Participants in the International Anti-Euthanasia Task Force include individuals from five continents concerned with disability rights, medicine, ethics, religion, law, education, and advocacy. The group opposes voluntary euthanasia and assisted suicide and attempts to protect groups it feels are medically vulnerable, especially elderly and disabled individuals. It provides information on euthanasia, suicide, assisted suicide, and related issues.

National Right to Life Committee
419 Seventh St. NW, Suite 5000
Washington, DC 20004-2293
(202) 626-8800

The National Right to Life Committee is a group that opposes abortion, euthanasia, and infanticide. It conducts research, supports counseling programs, lobbies before Congress, and distributes materials to the public on these issues. The committee has a library of more than four hundred books and over sixteen hundred pamphlets and clippings.

TASH: The Association for Persons with Severe Handicaps
11201 Greenwood Ave. N
Seattle, WA 98133
(206) 361-8870

TASH, founded in 1973, is an independent organization of people involved in all areas of service to the disabled. It seeks to ensure an independent, dignified lifestyle for all people with severe disabilities. The association provides current information on research findings, trends, and practices involving the severely disabled.

Suggestions for Further Reading

Frank Beckwith and Norman Giesler, *Matters of Life and Death: Calm Answers to Tough Questions About Abortion and Euthanasia.* Grand Rapids, MI: Baker Books, 1991.

Michael Biskup and Carol Wekesser, eds., *Suicide.* San Diego: Greenhaven Press, 1992.

Judith Bisnignano, *Living with Death.* Inverness, CA: Bartholomew Press, 1991.

Edward F. Dolan Jr., *Matters of Life and Death.* New York: Franklin Watts, 1981.

William Dudley, ed., *Death and Dying.* San Diego: Greenhaven Press, 1992.

Derek Humphry and Ann Wickett, *The Right to Die: Understanding Euthanasia.* New York: Harper & Row, 1986.

Jean Knox, *Death and Dying.* New York: Chelsea House, 1989.

William Maestri, *Choose Life and Not Death: A Primer on Abortion, Euthanasia, and Suicide.* New York: Alba, 1986.

La Verne Miley, *Euthanasia: Mercy or Murder?* Nashville, TN: Randall House, 1981.

Ann E. Weiss, *Bioethics: Dilemmas in Modern Medicine.* Hillside, NJ: Enslow Publishers, 1985.

Additional Works Consulted

Christiaan Barnard, *Good Life Good Death: A Doctor's Case for Euthanasia and Suicide*. Englewood Cliffs, NJ: Prentice-Hall, 1980.

Beverly Beyette, "The Reluctant Survivor," *Los Angeles Times*, September 13, 1992.

Victor Cohn, "The Right to Die: How Courts Have Ruled," *The Washington Post*, March 22, 1988.

B. D. Colen, *Karen Ann Quinlan: Dying in the Age of Eternal Life*. New York: Nash, 1976.

Craig Crosby, "Internists Grapple with How They Should Respond to Requests for Aid in Dying," *The Internist*, March 1992.

Maurice A. M. de Wachter, "Euthanasia in the Netherlands," *Hastings Center Report*, March/April 1992.

Diane M. Gianelli, "Debate Rages over MD-Aided Suicide," *American Medical News*, June 22, 1990.

Nancy Gibbs, "Mercy's Friend or Foe?" *Time*, December 28, 1992.

———, "Rx for Death," *Time*, May 31, 1993.

Denise Grady, "The Doctor Decided on Death," *Time*, February 15, 1988.

John Horgan, "Death with Dignity: The Dutch Explore the Limits of a Patient's Right to Die," *Scientific American*, March 1991.

Paul Jacobs, "Quietly, Doctors Already Help Terminal Patients Die," *Los Angeles Times*, September 29, 1992.

Tamara Jones, "Setting a Date for Death," *Los Angeles Times*, March 14, 1993.

Richard Knox, "Dutch Study Reports Euthanasia Practiced Widely but Cautiously," *The Boston Globe*, September 13, 1991.

———, "1 in 5 Doctors Say They Assisted a Patient's Death, Survey Finds," *The Boston Globe*, February 23, 1993.

———, "Poll: Americans Favor Mercy Killing," *The Boston Globe*, November 3, 1991.

Marvin Kohl, ed., *Beneficent Euthanasia*. Buffalo: Prometheus Books, 1975.

Ronald Kotulak, "The Big Hurt: Doctors Finally Start Listening to Our Cries of Pain," *The Chicago Tribune Magazine*, April 26, 1992.

Timothy J. Lace and Samuel F. Hunter, "Should Doctors Take Part in Planned Suicides?" *Journal of the American Medical Association*, December 1, 1989.

Gerald A. Larue, *Euthanasia and Religion: A Survey of the Attitudes of World Religions to the Right-to-Die*. Los Angeles: The Hemlock Society, 1985.

Jeff Lyon, *Playing God in the Nursery*. New York: W. W. Norton, 1985.

Daniel C. Maguire, *Death by Choice*. New York: Doubleday, 1974.

Gary E. McCuen and Theresa Boucher, *Terminating Life: Conflicting Values in Health Care*. Hudson, WI: Gem Publications, 1985.

Tom Morganthaue, Todd Barrett, and Frank Washington, "Dr. Kevorkian's Death Wish," *Newsweek*, March 8, 1993.

The New York Times, "A Jury's Sympathy with Suicide," May 6, 1994.

————, "Mercy for the Dying," May 28, 1994.

David Orntlicher, "Physician Participation in Assisted Suicide," *Journal of the American Medical Association*, October 6, 1989.

Frank A. Oski, M.D., "Opting Out," *The Nation*, January 24, 1994.

President's Commission for the Study of Ethical Problems in Medicine and Biomedical and Behavioral Research, *Deciding to Forego Life-Sustaining Treatment*. Washington, DC: U.S. Government Printing Office, 1983.

Robert Risley, "Mercy or Murder?" *Palm Beach Post*, May 1, 1988.

Betty Rollin, "The Politics of Mercy," *Family Circle*, April 24, 1994.

Sacred Congregation for the Doctrine of the Faith, "Declaration on Euthanasia," May 5, 1980. Available from The American Life League, Stafford, VA.

Earl E. Shelp, *Born to Die? Deciding the Fate of Critically Ill Newborns*. New York: The Free Press, 1986.

Time, "Victory for Dr. Death," August 3, 1992.

Earl Ubell, "Should Death Be a Patient's Choice?" *Parade*, February 9, 1992.

Pamela Warrick, "Suicide's Partner," *Los Angeles Times*, December 6, 1992.

Richard L. Worsnop, "Assisted Suicide," *CQ Researcher*, February 21, 1992.

Index

About the Author

For many years a junior high school reading teacher, Sunni Bloyd is now an award-winning, full-time writer and managing editor of the *Kings County Independent* newspaper in California. She is the author of numerous magazine articles and several books, among them *Endangered Species* and *Animal Rights*, published as part of the Lucent Overview Series.

Bloyd earned a B.A. from the University of California at Davis and a master's degree in education from the University of Dayton in Ohio. She and her husband live on a farm in central California with a number of cats, a horse, and an Australian shepherd named Dolly.

Picture Credits

Cover photo: © Rick Brady/Uniphoto
AP/Wide World Photos, 19, 33, 35, 38, 51, 59, 69, 70, 71, 77, 79
© Ron Chapple/FPG International, 102
© 1994 Gigi Cohen/Impact Visuals, 8
© Dennis Cox/SABA, 72
© 1989 Tom Ferentz/Impact Visuals, 27
© Spencer Grant/FPG International, 11
© Gregory Foster/Liaison International, 47
© Mark Harmel/FPG International, 109
© 1992 Marty Heitner/Impact Visuals, 99
© 1989 Ansell Horn/Impact Visuals, 105
© Dan Lamont 1991/Matrix, 93
© Brad Markel/Liaison International, 44
© 1992 Alain McLaughlin/Impact Visuals, 100
© Jeffry W. Myers/FPG International, 36
National Archives, 49
© O'Brien & Mayor Photography/FPG International, 12
© Barbara Peacock/FPG International, 42
© Bill Pugliano/Liaison International, 28, 62, 82
© Terry Qing/FPG International, 21
Reuters/Bettmann, 26, 66, 88, 90, 94
© Michael Rothwell/FPG International, 60
© Lonny Shavelson/Impact Visuals, 86
UPI/Bettmann, 30, 34, 52
© 1993 Jim West/Impact Visuals, 107
© Jim Whitmer/FPG International, 14
© Stan Willard/FPG International, 16